Leading through Strategy

*How Business Principles Can Help
Independent Schools Thrive.*

Thomas P. Olverson

ISBN: 978-1-962624-99-2

Table of Contents

Chapter 1: Prologue   5

Chapter 2: "A Plan is Not a Strategy"   10

Chapter 3: Setting the Stage: A Steep Hill to Climb   31

Chapter 4: Vision: "A Winning Aspiration"   47

Chapter 5: Strategy with the Customer in Mind   68

Chapter 6: Strategy: How Will You Win?   91

Chapter 7: Execution: Where Strategic Plans Go to Die   106

Chapter 8: Leadership Is More Than Strategy   130

Chapter 9: Epilogue   150

Afterword   161

Acknowledgments   163

About the Author   165

Chapter 1

Prologue

It was past 11 pm in August. I was by myself, struggling with the creation of goals for a strategic plan. The dining room table was strewn with paper — interview notes, spreadsheets with statistics, and recently discarded bad ideas.

I was six weeks into my tenure as the head at The Rivers School outside of Boston. I had learned a lot in those six weeks, studying the history of the school, analyzing data, and reflecting on my interviews with various stakeholders.

Despite my desire to focus on making sense of what I had learned, my mind wandered. "Well, you know Rivers isn't Brimmer and May; it's not Milton Academy either for God's sake," a former administrator at Rivers told me over the phone. The call occurred when I was winding up my tenure at Seabury Hall on Maui. I was learning about my new school and the independent school landscape in the Boston area. It was May 1997, and in a few months, I would get on a plane and travel over 5000 miles to a new home. I disguised my ignorance, agreeing with the former head while thinking to myself, "What's Milton Academy? What's Brimmer and May?"

My mind continued to wander, dwelling on my Maui experience.

In 1995, my eighth year at Seabury Hall, I knew it was time to start looking for a new job. My parents were getting older, and my father's declining health was of particular concern. My wife's widowed mother was in her late 80s, still living alone. We needed to get closer to our respective homes.

My family loved Maui. My daughter still claims it as home, having spent most of her childhood there and graduating from Seabury in 1997. Going to college on the East Coast, she was skeptical of our move to Boston. "Why are you following me?" Waiting to board the plane that would take her away from her home, she sobbed. We all did. Maui is magical.

I started my headship at Seabury in 1987 when I was 34 years old. I had been looking for a senior administrative position the previous two years when a friend sent me the advertisement for the Seabury headship: "You should apply, Tom. You won't get the job, but you may get a free trip to Maui." That sounded good so I applied. I met with three trustees in New Orleans in the early fall of 1986, and they liked me enough to invite my wife and me out to Maui for four days, two of which would be focused on interviews and the other two on enjoying the beautiful island. All expenses paid. Throughout the process, I never thought I would be selected so I never even considered the possibility of moving to Maui. On the last two days, my wife and I were put up in a luxury condo right on Makena Beach, owned by one of the trustees. The beach was beautiful, the ocean warm, and the sunsets colorful.

Two weeks later I was offered the job.

"WHAT!!!!"

My wife and I talked it over. We couldn't move to Maui; nobody moves to Maui. But we couldn't turn this job down, not after the warm Aloha spirit the trustees showed us while visiting. I said, "yes."

Sitting alone at that dining room table, I tried to get back to the task at hand - strategic goals for Rivers. However, my wandering mind continued to win the day. I thought of the several schools that invited me for interviews in 1995-6 in my quest to return to the mainland. They were all excellent schools with national reputations, schools that would allow me to puff my chest out a little and proudly display one of their names on my badge at the NAIS Conference. At some point, they would look at the badge; they all do. But only in a couple of cases did I advance to the finalist round; each time I came up short.

What a blessing! Do you ever think about God having a plan for you? Much of my life has pitted my desires (the prestige that comes from heading a "great" school) against God's plan for me (where will your talents make the most significant difference?). It was a war that led to self-doubt, a sense of inferiority, and anger. It was a war I lost. "THANK YOU, GOD."

I would have loved the name-tag status of a nationally well-known school, the money, the deferred compensation, and the mega-capital campaigns:

Jack, NAIS Conference Fellow Head: **"Tom, how's it going?"**

Tom: **"Jack, I have been so busy! We reached our goal of $80 million in the capital campaign, and can you believe it? The Board has decided to reset the goal to $100 million."**

Jack: **"Wow! That is so impressive, Tom. Congratulations! Have you ever considered joining the Headmasters' Association?"**

Toward the end of the brief conversation, Jack's eyes wander, signaling the end of the conversation and the hunt for fresh "networking" opportunities.

But God knew before I knew that I am an entrepreneur at heart. Change is in my DNA; the challenge of adding substantial value to a school gets my creative juices going, an opportunity to create my personal art. If I could go back and talk to my former students and advisees, I would tell them never to pass up the opportunity to do their own art. It may be as simple and profound as coaching a little league team, leading an organization, or volunteering at church. But it has to be something you can bring your whole self to – intelligence, personality, creativity, and passion. Martha Graham wrote:

> There is a vitality, a life force, an energy, a quickening that is translated through you into action, and because there is only one of you in all of time, this expression is unique. And if you block it, it will never exist through any other medium, and it will be lost. The world will not have it. It is not your business to determine how good it is nor how valuable nor how it compares with other expressions. It is your business to keep it yours clearly and directly, to keep the channel open. You do not even have to believe in yourself or your work. You have to keep yourself open and aware to the urges that motivate you. Keep the channel open.

I am certain God looked at my quest for fame and fortune and just shook Her head: "Will this guy ever get it?" At our core, we humans really are silly. We can only thank God that God doesn't hold that against us.

The wandering mind begins to lose steam. The strategic goals will have to wait. Time for bed.

Chapter 2

"A Plan is Not a Strategy"

In a You Tube video, Roger Martin states, "a plan is not a strategy." His statement is an invitation to take a journey that can change the way you lead.

Three years into my new career as an independent school consultant, I read *Playing to Win* by Roger Martin and A.G. Lafley. I was excited to read this book about strategy because Martin had been a senior consultant at the Monitor Group, a world-renowned business consulting firm headquartered in Cambridge, Massachusetts. For nine years while head at The Rivers School, I was able to tap into the knowledge of one of Monitor's leading strategic marketing consultants, thanks to the efforts of a Rivers trustee. Monitor grew out of Harvard Business School and had Michael Porter, one of the preeminent organizational strategists in the world, as one of its founders. Lafley had been the CEO of Procter & Gamble, and many of the illustrations in the book came from his P&G experience.

As I read the book, I realized I had used the same principles in developing strategy at Rivers. More specifically, I used the same thinking. Of course, I could not recreate the genius of Martin and Lafley, but the same kind of thinking, the same critical questions, and the way they intersected with each other were top-of-mind as I began working on a strategic plan for Rivers. Reading *Playing to Win* was a huge "*aha*" moment, an opportunity to pull together and give structure to thinking that I intuitively used in writing the Rivers strategic plan.

As I pondered the ideas in *Playing to Win*, post my Rivers experience, I became acutely aware of the inadequacies of strategic planning for independent schools. Throughout my career, I had talked to several heads disappointed in the results of their strategic planning process, often after the significant expense of a consultant. The joke about pulling the strategic plan off the shelf when the visiting accreditation committee came had become stale. I became more convinced that strategic planning was a lost opportunity because schools used a superficial process that required little thinking and even less imagination.

Strategic plans can be effective tools for charting the course for a school's future, getting key stakeholders on the same page, and appropriately allocating time, energy, and resources to help the school do a better job living its mission. But despite these potential benefits, I confess that I often cringe when I hear a head of school talk about beginning the strategic planning process.

Why does strategic planning fail for many independent schools? Below are six reasons.

1. **There is no vision.** Formulating a strategy is about creating a roadmap, but the roadmap has to lead somewhere. The absence of a vision means that many strategic plans are generic, bland copies of what other schools are doing and devoid of any deep thinking about the school's mission, market opportunities,

aspirations, and institutional capabilities. Creating a vision, one that inspires stakeholders, is hard work. When I visit independent schools, its absence is often the most glaring deficiency. And even when vision is present, it is often the result of shallow thinking, mindless adoption of the work of other schools, and a failure to think creatively about how to integrate the mission, history, and culture of the school with the realities of the marketplace.

2. **Solving problems becomes a substitute for creating a future.** This deficiency is a logical outcome of the absence of vision. When there is no North Star, the easy default is to solve perceived problems, starting with the ones seen as the biggest. How many times in the past decade have I read a strategic plan that has financial sustainability as a major strategic goal? Far too many! Please, heads and trustees, do not make financial sustainability a strategic goal. It inspires no one. Do you think parents want to hear that the school's leadership is focused on alternative revenue? Financial sustainability is the *result* of achieving something great in the marketplace, something of real value. It should be the consequence of realizing a great vision. It is not a strategy.

3. **Many strategic plans fail to account for the school's capacity to execute the plan.** Rob Evans made this point in his magnificent article, *"The Case against Strategic Planning."* Establishing strategic goals in the absence of critical thinking about the school's capacity to execute these goals seems like a fool's errand. Schools set themselves up for disappointment

and cynicism because they refuse to think about limitations and assets as essential elements in determining the strategic goals. Heads also fail to see successful execution as a means to create expanded capabilities that allow for further school improvement. Executing strategy (what to do and in what sequence) should create a virtuous cycle, which means a desired result and greater capacity for implementing more initiatives in the future. It's like a superior chess player, able to envision two or three moves ahead.

4. **Most strategic plans suffer from too much detail.** Critical to achieving buy-in for a strategic plan is the opportunity for talented administrators and faculty to use their individual and collective imaginations to help the school achieve its goals. When the strategic planning committee or the head of school details the steps to realize specific goals, it becomes another form of top-down management, ripe for unenthusiastic participation and at worse, cynicism.

One head of school communicated to his faculty and administrators through words and actions the following: "Here is the sandbox you get to play in. Within that sandbox, I want you to be as creative as you can be; I want you to talk about initiatives that will make that sandbox a special place. However, you can only play in this sandbox; you can't play in the one next to it." In drawing on the imaginations of the faculty and administrators, he created buy-in but made clear the existence of guardrails. In addition, the implementation of strategy must be linked to results. When the desired results don't come about, there is an opportunity to learn and to make critical adjustments. Checking off a bunch of tasks without determining if those tasks are helping the school realize the vision is mindless discipline overwhelming the promise of meaningful change.

5. **Too many strategic plans fail to factor in the realities of the marketplace.** Please, don't get me wrong; ultimately, the purpose of a strategic plan is to help the school do a better job of living its mission. But with a high percentage of independent schools losing enrollment over the last ten years (notwithstanding the jump associated with the pandemic), it is imperative that heads and trustees create plans that will also help them win in the market. Choosing between mission and market is not an option. The realization of the vision as outlined in the strategy should strengthen the school's position in the market as well as serve the mission. But make no mistake; the "either-or" forces can be formidable. Powerful, veteran teachers, long-serving board members, a strong alumni body, a stagnant culture — these all make it easy to disdain the realities of the market in order to preserve institutional tradition.

6. **Heads are not trained to be good strategic thinkers.** At a time of declining enrollment and softening demand (again, notwithstanding the bump that came with the pandemic), it is easy to blame trustees for the failure of strategic initiatives. But more significantly, heads are poorly prepared to lead a strategic planning process because they have little or no training in strategic

thinking. Rarely are first-time heads taught how to objectively dissect their schools, gain insights into the nature of the market, and understand the school's assets and limitations in executing a plan. The key elements of a strategy represent a system: vision, target audience, strategy, institutional capabilities, and structures. Most independent schools' strategic plans represent a list of things they should do. There is no coherence, no connection to the brand the school wishes to build or strengthen. (Olverson, January 2019, RG 175 Blog)

Many of the above observations come from my application of Martin and Lafley's work to independent schools. I am inspired to write this book to show how their thinking can be applied to an independent school and produce stunning results. When I look back on my tenure at Rivers, my first reaction is to point to some program or a couple of key moments as primary reasons for success. And to be honest, luck played a role in the turnaround of the school. But most importantly, Rivers' success came from a way of thinking about change and the future, looking at how the critical components fit together to create a virtuous cycle, understanding the risks and rewards of each strategy, and most importantly, tapping into the collective imagination of talented people who want to achieve something big.

From reading their book, you will see that Martin and Lafley's approach to strategic planning is anything but cookie-cutter. To take their journey, you have to ask hard questions of yourself and others. You have to use your imagination. You have to make *choices*. You have to have the courage to commit to a strategy that you can't be positive will work. No wonder educational leaders have a difficult time thinking strategically. We educators like certainty. For the most part, risk-taking is not in our DNA.

Moreover, the clear assumption in *Playing to Win* is that strategy is about gaining a competitive advantage, winning in the marketplace, and building or strengthening a brand that will drive customers to the business. This marketing orientation is just not a part of the mindset of most current and aspiring heads as well as trustees. It's no wonder so many schools, suffering from enrollment challenges, stay stuck in the quicksand.

You might ask, "What about wealthy schools? Why should they be concerned about owning a market niche?" It's a fair question since many of them already own a market niche. This book is not for heads at these kinds of schools. Wealthy schools can flounder under poor leadership, but the lasting damage is usually minimal. Money proves to be the great insulator, protecting the school from incapable heads and boards.

This book is for those independent school leaders who have to play a game they can lose and who may very well be motivated by the fact that they can lose. I have read somewhere that it's not that entrepreneurs love risk; it's just that they can tolerate more of it than others. In my strategic world, risks are a given. I fervently believe you can always "learn" your way out of a wrong turn. But if you are risk-averse, think twice about leading a school that needs to change in significant ways.

Playing to Win details five critical questions that constitute real strategic thinking:

1. What is your winning aspiration?
2. Where do you want to play?
3. How will you win?
4. What are the capabilities of the organization?
5. What structures are needed to achieve the goals?

Martin and Lafley make two critical points in explaining the significance of these five questions. First, an organization cannot answer any of these questions without determining how the answer will impact the answers to the other four questions. To use a simple illustration, a school establishes a goal of raising $100 million, but it is a ridiculous goal because the school lacks the resources (capabilities) to achieve such a lofty goal.

The second point is equally important. Because *Playing to Win* was intended for profit-making businesses, it was naturally focused on gaining a competitive advantage in the marketplace. As I pondered the application of this idea to the school business, I initially thought the concept of competitive advantage was too narrow for schools developing a strategic plan. I reverted to the standard strategic planning framework: program, people, and facilities. But the more I thought about it, the more I came to believe that for most schools, developing strategy by using the enrollment management portal has significant upside and can easily incorporate program, people, and facilities. In short, strengthening your school's market position should be the goal of independent school strategic planning. It provides the most powerful lens to ultimately add value to your school.

Furthermore, in the school business, the stronger the brand, the greater the capacity for future fundraising. As it turns out, Martin and Lafley's focus on competitive advantage should not be dismissed; it should be embraced, even by a non-profit independent school. It's true that the mission of the school should be central to decision-making. However, schools that do strategic planning without the intent of gaining a competitive advantage are seriously handicapping the potential for positive change.

Naturally, gaining a competitive advantage raises the question, "What if there are no competitors?" If strategy is about gaining a competitive advantage, the absence of competitors poses a significant challenge for an independent school. In what arenas does the school compete? Where will its greatness lie? Competition helps a school understand context and the landscape of reality; it focuses attention. Competition leads to clarifying goals, creating priorities, and properly sequencing efforts. It provides a yardstick for measuring performance. Without it, there's just a vacuum, and vacuums are seldom an effective repository for creativity. And yet, even if the competition is the local public school system, it is imperative for an independent school to see it as the competition.

One independent school competing athletically against several bigger public schools, and holding its own, was offered the opportunity to join a "small school league." The school jumped at the chance, and I was shocked when I heard it had done so. If a school is succeeding athletically against schools four times its size, what strategic value is there in dropping down to a league that will lack relevance? How will it know how good its program really is? How will the decision affect admissions? It was a classic path of least resistance, a decision that I thought would gradually diminish the importance of athletics at the school. Seek out competition; indeed, find a worthy enemy, one that can make your school better.

This book includes six short chapters besides this introduction, the prologue, and an epilogue. There are questions and a space for notes after most chapters so that readers might jot down thoughts related to their own respective circumstances. The next chapter provides the reader with some context about The Rivers School, a sort of abbreviated SWOT (Strength, Weaknesses, Opportunities, Threats) analysis I conducted in 1997 when I arrived. Rod Snelling, the founder of Independent School Management, fervently believed that every school embarking on strategic planning should first go through what he called an institutional assessment. Rod's assessment was organized differently from a SWOT, but the result was the same — an analysis of the current reality of the school through the examination of data and the establishment of broad themes based on interviews with many stakeholders. Rod's insistence on an institutional assessment was spot-on. Without a systematic and often painful assessment of the school's current condition, generating a relevant and compelling vision for the school is impossible. Granted, it is easy to fall into the trap of using the assessment to create a strategic plan that solves a bunch of problems, big and small. And to be sure, many independent school strategic plans are just proposed solutions to perceived problems. Real strategic thinking, however, demands that the identification of problems is merely a prelude to creating a vision that will do more than just solve problems; it will inspire community members to create something special, something bigger than any one person. It will unleash creativity.

The following four chapters will apply Martin and Lafley's five questions to my experience at Rivers as well as my observations of other schools. I combined the questions on capability and systems into one chapter under the heading of execution. By showing the application of all five key concepts in my own experience, I hope that you can use a similar approach as you set a strategic direction for your school. Above all else, I want you to understand the research and deep analysis required to develop strategy and the importance of honing thinking skills that will lead to insights about where the school is now, where it can be in the future, and how it can get there. This is hard work, work that should not be outsourced to a consultant, as is the habit of so many schools. A consultant can help by providing guidance on how to take the journey, but she should not hand the head a distilled set of findings and a vision. The head should never outsource the chance for deep learning.

After examining the application of Martin and Lafley's concepts, I include a sixth chapter, which discusses key leadership qualities associated with devising and implementing strategy. Finally, I have included an epilogue of information and data showing the impact of strategic thinking on Rivers.

Throughout the book there is a commitment to the unvarnished truth and a willingness to "live the questions," as Rainer Maria Rilke so profoundly and beautifully wrote. Once school leadership grasps reality, it is liberated to make decisions that can truly change the direction of a school and the lives of its students. As you will see, this is easier said than done. Mythologies and outdated narratives often define a school's culture and set limits on what can and cannot be done. No head wants to share negatives with the board. But piercing these mythologies can be a painful but often crucial first step in school improvement.

One school I worked with had a clear path to a brand of excellence, a goal that trustees and staff both desired. However, within the faculty, a narrative had been born in the absence of a clear school purpose: "we meet students where they are." There is absolutely nothing wrong with this sentiment except that it does not align with the student pursuit of excellence. At this school though, it was a powerful driver of behavior, a norm followed by much of the faculty, no matter their stated desires for student excellence. The head has yet to address the issue but knows it needs attention. Here's where the political skills of an effective head come into play. Faculty culture can represent dangerous terrain. Addressing the issue directly may lead to a backlash, which, in turn, may undermine the change efforts. The head's capacity to "read the audience," seek advice, and choose a strategy that will allow the faculty to see the contradiction without getting defensive — all of these actions can be crucial to success. Effective heads of school have high EQ (Emotional Quotient); their sixth sense tells them there could be danger down the road as they tackle complex challenges.

You may be wondering if I accessed the wisdom of fellow heads in the Boston area while I was at Rivers. I did not. Of course, there were some very intelligent, highly capable heads in the ISL (Independent School League) and at some of the other wonderful schools in the area. But there were two significant barriers. First, the competition for students was so intense in Boston that it was difficult for heads to drop their guards and be transparent. Even as we met three times a year at the Harvard Club, I found the conversations anything but transparent. Second, these heads ran successful schools with generally strong brands. None of them were entrepreneurs. Many thought in similar ways —somewhat formulaic and often with an eye focused on what elite colleges and other highly-regarded prep schools were doing.

However, I did have people I could lean on for advice, and all of them came from the business world. Smart, savvy, and incredibly knowledgeable, many of them were trustees. One trustee, one of the original members of the Monitor Group, saw the complexity of the school's marketing challenges. He expressed his desire to focus on marketing, but only under the condition that the person who led the effort must know what she was talking about. In his mind, nonprofit boards are filled with well-meaning folks who have no idea what they are doing when it comes to governance. So, this trustee combed Monitor for a leading marketing strategist, and he hit a home run! Our new-found consultant advised *Fortune 500* companies and had written a cover article on innovation for *Harvard Business Review.* Our trustee's power of persuasion was simple: "Don't you get tired of working for *Fortune 500* companies all the time?" The star consultant was sold, and Rivers would pay him nothing. We called ourselves the Marketing Committee, but the meetings consisted of the consultant extracting information from us, seeing connections, and structuring and prioritizing our efforts. I can't really point to a specific strategy that came from this group, but significantly, the consultant taught us how to think as a marketing strategist does, which, in retrospect, helped me to understand more concretely what I had only intuited seven years earlier when I wrote the strategic plan. It forced me to go further and deeper in my understanding of the customer perspective.

Yes, I was incredibly fortunate to have access to some talented and knowledgeable experts. You might think that access to this kind of talent is going to be impossible for your school. But herein lies my purpose in writing the book. My hope is that you can learn what questions to ask, how to frame your strategic challenges, and most importantly, how to think about them logically and creatively. In 1997, as I pondered the vision and strategic goals for Rivers, my thinking was on the right track, but I lacked the structured framework that Martin and Lafley created sixteen years later. My approach was more intuitive. My goal is that after reading this book, you will have the benefit of their wisdom as it applies to independent schools.

But a framework does not preclude hard work. If you are to gain any value from this approach, you will have to think deeper and harder than you ever have. In my first two years at Rivers, I arrived at school by 5:45 am each work day and spent the next hour and a half sipping coffee and thinking:

1. What market niche can Rivers own?
2. How do we leverage our music school?
3. How do we attract better athletes?
4. How do I navigate the change process so I don't have to face a wall of resistance?
5. What personnel moves do I need to make in order to maximize the school's potential?
6. How do I incentivize teacher excellence and still maintain high faculty morale?
7. Where can I get money to jumpstart change?

These are just a handful of questions I grappled with. The genius of Martin and Lafley is that they have given structure to my intuition.

It is essential that you do not mindlessly copy the actions I took at Rivers. In doing so, you would be committing a different form of the same mistake so many independent schools make – planning without thought and imagination. Once you start asking the right questions relevant to your school and wrestle with them in a way that leads to a strategy that will create value, you have set the table for success. The answers I came up with at Rivers should be irrelevant to you. Only the questions and the deep thinking that results from struggling with them can lead to insights that will translate into appropriate action for your school. Focus on the questions, not the answers. Focus on your school and its particular circumstances.

By way of example, in working with a school in a relatively small town in the South, I have taken great pains to understand the school's context and its assets and limitations before having meaningful conversations about strategy with the head. Given the limited population the school serves, the head and I concluded that closely monitoring tuition levels is crucial to the school's continuing to thrive and maintain full enrollment. Conversely, adding "bells and whistles" is a bad strategy and would represent a mindless imitation of what the big-city schools were doing. A drop in enrollment could lead to the elimination of football, which is the kiss of death in the South. The key to winning for this school is to beat the public school by five touchdowns in key programs that families value. For example, ensuring that this school's test scores are vastly superior to those of the public schools is essential. Adding a center for teacher innovation is not. Given this particular context, playing the existing game as opposed to creating a whole new marketing category is the winning strategy. The strategy this school developed arose from the particular context in which it found itself. The school asked the same questions I asked at Rivers; it just came up with very different answers. (Olverson, October 2017, RG 175 Blog)

One other advisor accelerated my learning. He was the chair of the Rivers math department. He pursued his passion for teaching after selling his last start-up company. Everyone in the Rivers community understood his impact on students. However, few knew of his impact on my thinking. Having started four technology businesses, two of which hit the jackpot, he was an entrepreneur through and through. He taught me the importance of thinking like a customer and designing student experiences that would launch positive word-of-mouth. We spent hours talking about business and marketing. The last time I saw him, we were at Fenway Park, watching the Red Sox. We talked business throughout the whole game. The lady behind us asked, "Hey, are you guys ever going to watch the game? You've been yakking the whole time." His counsel along with that of other key advisors illustrates a key point: a "kitchen cabinet" of talented, intelligent people, whose agenda is nothing more than your success and the success of the school, is one of the most powerful assets you can have.

At this point, I am sure you have asked yourself why I worked by myself on the strategic goals. It's certainly an appropriate question given that the beginning stages of a strategic planning process often include gathering trustees and senior administrators, maybe key parent leaders and alumni, all led by a consultant who divides the larger group into smaller groups with specific tasks. By the end of the day, "Voila," the school has its strategic goals, even if the specific objectives may take months to establish. The process is collaborative and inclusive and therefore, will meet with the approving eyes of the visiting accreditation team. In addition, the process includes a diversity of opinions, which all the management gurus claim is critical for better decisions. But I find this process shallow. It is strategic planning at its worst — a plan without a strategy.

More specifically, for the challenges Rivers faced, an inclusive process did not feel appropriate. I already knew that the capacity to implement goals at Rivers would be stretched to the limit. Setting priorities and maintaining focus would be instrumental in achieving success. I didn't want to spend time implementing someone else's agenda, not because I wanted to hoard power but because the school could not afford to dilute its efforts to satisfy key stakeholders. It did not have the resources. In these circumstances, shared decision-making felt like politics to me. The school needed logic and coherence to drive change, not the whims of wealthy trustees or popular administrators. Yes, I wanted to control the narrative and set the strategic priorities. And I was willing to take the heat. What I did not want was a watered-down political document.

My approach raises the question of shared decision-making and collaboration, two important facets of organizational culture. But not always. Too many strategic decisions in independent schools are made by people with little knowledge of the topics at hand. Perhaps the head has unwittingly forfeited power, or the board has failed to tap the expertise of trustees to address challenges in which they can add real expertise to the conversation. In my mind, being a successful head is in part, about exercising power and giving power away, and knowing under what circumstances to do each one. Otherwise, process triumphs over outcomes. Process is important, but I want a process that leads to the desired outcomes, not a series of feel-good moments when everyone is heard, and nothing of consequence is achieved. When the Monitor consultant who worked with Rivers for nine years met with us, the external senior administrators and I let him completely run the meeting. We listened, answered his questions, brought him data, and learned. We willingly deferred to someone with far more expertise than we had.

Eschewing the typical inclusive process, I took a different approach. I created the strategic goals and then spent the year getting people on board. I took a lot of steps forward and a lot of steps backward during that year, but intuitively, I knew that if the school was going to become a player in the ISL, it had to focus its time, energy, attention, and money on creating something of value. A political strategy where everybody gets something was not going to get it done.

Today, I would never advise a head to create a strategic plan by herself. I have learned ways to work with trustees, administrators, and faculty to generate ideas that naturally flow from the SWOT analysis and the establishment of a vision. Because the head controls the substance of the SWOT analysis, critical, well-chosen points can be made to help incline the trustees to develop goals that align with the head's vision. In addition, the head's vision is not only a generator of ideas but also an anchor that tethers strategic goals to it. There has to be a logical connection between the vision and the goals, and the head can use this connection to maintain focus.

In no way do I want the reader to think that I brought the same level of sophistication to my Rivers experience as Martin and Lafley brought to Procter & Gamble. *Playing to Win* offers a logical, nuanced, and detailed approach to strategy that only two intelligent, skilled, and experienced leaders in the business world could provide. The intent of this book is to show the power of Martin and Lafley's concepts to help school leaders use strategy to bring about sustainable change in a school.

Please note that, my use of some broad business concepts and language is not intended to be dismissive of mission. Embedded in mission are the dreams and aspirations of the organization. But independent schools must stop pitting their missions against the realities of the market. They need to disdain the false either-or choice and use their imaginations to create visions that are truly "winning aspirations." As the book will show, this is hard but necessary work.

Finally, several ideas and examples in the book come directly from my blog posts on the RG 175 website. This book has encouraged me to pull together these ideas and examples and combine them to create a deeper, more comprehensive understanding of strategy and its use in the independent school world. Where appropriate, I have cited the blog posts.

Questions

1. Do you want to create a plan to solve problems or develop a strategy to realize a vision? What does your school need most and why?

2. Are there any short-term challenges that must be addressed before developing strategy?

3. What are the potential roadblocks to creating a strategy that focuses on capturing or solidifying a position in the market?

4. Who in your community has expertise that can be tapped in order to help you develop and realize a vision?

5. What are the politics of your situation, and how will you navigate them? Who has power, and how will you get them on board?

Reader's Notes

Chapter 3

Setting the Stage:
A Steep Hill to Climb

A SWOT analysis conducted by the new head of school can provide a rich source of information and perspective that prompts deep thinking about where the school is, potential aspirations for the future, and capabilities and structures necessary for success. The result of this analysis identifies the critical strategic questions and avoids the tendency to devise answers to questions that really don't matter. Because the SWOT involves interviews, it's also an effective way for new heads to begin developing relationships with key stakeholders.

In particular, the one-on-one sessions with trustees can provide a new head invaluable perspective on the values and priorities of these important stakeholders. If Trustee X thinks the athletic program needs major improvement, a head needs to know that information sooner rather than later. If Trustee Y, a major donor, believes that college counseling is weak, this is critical information as she and the head develop a relationship. In short, the interviews can provide perspective that allows the new head to navigate conversations and think about the possible zigs and zags she may need to take going forward.

But the most important reason for a new head to conduct a SWOT is to develop her own independent perspective of the school. As the new head begins to formulate impressions, she now has a basis for determining if key stakeholders are seeing what she is seeing. She can begin assessing the extent of the challenge to build consensus and effect change. For instance, in an effort to determine the quality of teaching, a new head may sit in on several classes to get to know the school's most important work. Although she is clear with teachers that she is not sitting in on their classes to evaluate them, she, nonetheless, will have some impressions about each teacher whose class she visits. With these impressions, the new head has an opportunity to test them with academic administrators to determine the degree of alignment. If the dean of faculty thinks that Ms. Jones is a great English teacher, and the new head sees her as mediocre at best, this variance is critical information for the new head to have. In the analysis of their respective schools, new heads have to identify potential barriers to change, including an absence of alignment, to ensure that their efforts will have the intended impact. Leaders who assume that if they decree it, it will happen, are living in a fantasy world.

But a new head's analysis of the school has further benefits.

I value humility in a leader. As an independent school search consultant, I associate humility with learning, and being a learner is one of the key qualities of effective leadership. Learners are curious. Leader-learners probe, look for insights, and value the opinions of others. Thus, a candidate referred to as the "smartest person in the room" is not someone I normally pursue for a headship. That application usually goes in the "no way" pile.

But under certain circumstances, I have seen the value of being the "expert." Let me explain by describing a composite of schools I have encountered over the last nine years.

XXY Academy has just hired a new head who started four months ago. The school has been struggling with enrollment since the 2008 financial crisis and during that time, has had three heads of school in addition to the new one. The school's enrollment has dropped from 1000 to 850 in the last fifteen years. The loss of students has impacted many facets of the school's operation, most notably teacher salaries, class size, and the athletic program. Trustees have a myriad of theories about why enrollment has not bounced back: 1) tuition is too high, 2) the football team is weak, 3) the school is not getting the "word" out, 4) the admissions director is ineffective, and more. Many trustees are exasperated as they have been espousing their respective theories for years to no effect. Each one knows something is wrong and supposedly knows how to fix it. They just need a head who "gets it." Most of the trustees are parents.

Enter the fictional Frank Smith, the new head of school, hired to solve the enrollment problem. Here is the reality behind the enrollment crisis Frank faces:

1. The balance of power is clearly with the board of trustees, as is the case with many leadership transitions in independent schools.

2. The board consists mostly of parents; thus, the trustees' judgment about the long-term sustainability of the school is clouded by the experience of their children — both positive and negative.

33

3. Trustee theories about the low enrollment are, at best, superficial and certainly not supported by data, much less a sophisticated interpretation of data.

In essence, Frank has a board with too much power, shaky judgment, and little knowledge of how to effectively address the enrollment challenge — not a group of people that should engender confidence in developing an effective plan. Add to this scenario the real possibility that Frank is a first-time head who came up through the academic ranks with little knowledge of working with a board.

Despite what you might think, Frank's first task is not to devise a plan to address the enrollment decline. Rather, it is to re-balance the power between administration and board while achieving some degree of consensus about the nexus of the problem. In short, Frank needs to *earn power* by demonstrating to the trustees that he knows what he is talking about, at least when it comes to understanding the real challenges the school is facing. This is a necessary prelude to getting the power brokers on the same page. Moving forward without a clear consensus about the real nature of the problem is a prescription for constant re-litigation. Quagmire wins.

In order to be the convincing expert, Frank must study the school, its history, its competition, as well as current and recent data. He must understand parent and faculty perspectives and the drivers and barriers associated with behavior in the market. Frank needs to present his SWOT analysis to the board, demonstrating that he has done his homework and speaks with a degree of authority. In doing so, he forces the board to think strategically, to ground decisions in data instead of the experiences of their children, and most importantly, to make the head a full partner, if not the leader, in devising strategies for creating value that will lead to an increase in enrollment. (Olverson, January 2023, RG 175 Blog)

Please note that I do not recommend that new heads constantly prove they are the most intelligent people in the room. However, early in their tenure, they must demonstrate their expertise in order to establish a healthier balance of power with their boards and create a foundation for real change by compelling trustees to adopt a strategic perspective.

You might think that a SWOT analysis is best left to a consultant in preparation for developing a strategic plan. Often, the school assessment is part of the consultant's package, and the work begins at the end of the head's first year or the beginning of the second. If a school wants to use this process, that's fine. However, the consultant's work should never be a substitute for the head's own deep analysis of the school. As mentioned above, that analysis can often engender confidence in the head's leadership once she presents her results to the board and faculty. In addition, the underlining drivers in future decision-making shift to the strategic. Furthermore, by doing her own analysis, the head begins to understand the political landscape as she receives feedback. She can assess the appetite for change and thus determine what necessary steps must be taken to set the stage for the establishment of a strategy.

By mid-August 1997, after seven weeks on the job, I had learned much about Rivers and independent schools in the Boston area. My learning was the result of extensive research. I interviewed all the Rivers administrators and staff, the trustees individually, and as many faculty as I could during the summer months. I pored over statistics and studied the history of the school. I read a particularly valuable capital campaign feasibility study completed by Marts and Lundy, a well-known fundraising consulting firm; I interviewed the lead consultant. I even talked with two educational consultants who placed students in secondary independent schools; I was hoping to gain an outside perspective on how prospective parents viewed Rivers.

I sought to establish an unvarnished perspective, believing that change would not happen until I truly understood this school — the good and the bad. I was not interested in "showing up" my predecessors by riding in on my white horse. I have seen new heads do this; it's repulsive. "Let's tear down the past so that I, as the new head, can show you the right way to lead the school out of the wilderness." It sounds like misguided missionary work to me. Not only is it disrespectful to those who came before, but it reveals an arrogance that rarely works to bring about positive and lasting change. Al Adams, in his brilliant articles on entering a school community as its new leader, wisely communicated the importance of bringing an attitude of respect to the study of a school and honoring the many contributions that its heroes made to help the school achieve whatever success it had up to that point. Truth, humility, gratitude, and not self-serving arrogance should drive the new leader's learning.

I learned that Rivers began as an open-air school in 1915. It was founded by a group of doctors who were not only concerned about the threat of tuberculosis but also felt strongly that breathing fresh air was critical to a healthy and productive life. Robert Rivers was the first head, and it was clear from some of his writings as well as student newspaper clippings, that he valued close relationships. Students liked to poke fun at him, chiding him for spending so much time on the golf course. I spent hours looking at the old photographs, and I was especially drawn to the ones with students bundled up in oversized coats and thick gloves, trying to hold on to their pencils with the windows wide-open in the dead of winter... in Boston. Talk about living your mission!

After a change of leadership in 1928, The Rivers School closed its windows. In my mind, this was a significant turning point in the school's history. It had lost its *raison d'être*. When I told community members this fact, I expected the "aha" moment that I had — vigorous nodding of the heads, signifying an understanding of the dramatic loss of the school's purpose for being and a new insight into why the school had floundered for seventy years after. Instead, I received polite, courteous smiles — certainly not the road-to-Damascus moment I had anticipated.

Rivers' seventy years of floundering had taken a cumulative toll. In 1997, the school lacked a clear identity. It reveled in its athletic association with some of the country's oldest, richest, most prestigious schools. But it stood out as a school most definitely lacking in wealth and prestige. Its de facto strategy was *status by association*.

Throughout the 80s and 90s, Rivers was the perennial doormat in the athletically competitive Independent School League (ISL). The vast majority of its male and female teams ended their respective seasons with losing records. In the early nineties, the head of school declared a headmaster's holiday because the boys soccer team won its first league game in three years.

The academic and admission profiles were no better — modest test scores, a high acceptance rate, increasing numbers of students who used the tutoring center, and a faculty that was both mediocre and uninspiring, with several notable exceptions.

As is the case at schools with similar profiles, Rivers developed narratives that put salve on its wounded ego: "Unlike other schools, our teachers deeply care about their students; we take students where they are and help them grow; Rivers believes in its students until they believe in themselves."

I don't want to be dismissive of these descriptors; there was just enough truth in each of them to justify the mythology. But they also served the purpose of stifling the hard work of getting better. The descriptors tried to hide the unspoken "good enough" culture that is a part of so many schools. To make a school or for that matter, any organization better, the leader has to identify the comfortable narratives that stakeholders use to shield themselves from the truth. In a few months, I would begin my de-mythologizing campaign, albeit with respect for the school's past, as a necessary prelude to change.

You might question why caring about students necessarily constitutes a mythology. I don't think it does. I have seen schools transform students, using the foundation of deep caring for the growth of children. But these schools proudly proclaim that this is the heart of their respective missions. They constantly look to improve their practices in service to this mission. Small classes, a great advisor program, world-class student support, and a faculty who live the mission are hallmarks of great schools that are less concerned about the college placement list and more concerned about the personal growth of their students. Bravo!

But Rivers was not one of these schools. It envied the more prestigious schools in the ISL; there was no evidence that it embraced the kinds of students attending the school. My research uncovered nothing that indicated a commitment to professional growth that would lead teachers to better, more authentic ways to help these kinds of students truly grow. A department head told me that veteran teachers often gave students low grades at the beginning of the year and higher grades at the end of the year. It was a sham. There was no real student growth, greater competency, and more developed skills — just a higher grade. Her frustration was magnified by parents attributing their students' success to the teacher. How else could Johnny begin as a C- student and end as a B+ student?

The facilities at Rivers in 1997 reflected its lowly status — ugly, limited, and outdated. When it rained, the maintenance crew had to lay six-foot tables in front of the entrances to some of the buildings because the water pooled up. I was embarrassed as I watched student tour guides lead prospective families into a building by first stepping on the bridge-table. The bottom floor of the science building was constantly flooding. The gym floor (not wood) was dangerous because players kept slipping on it. Drama productions were performed in the dining/assembly hall, with almost no wing space and no place to store props or sets. There was no hockey rink, even though the school had a boys' hockey team. Going to away games at Groton, Middlesex, Nobles, and all the other schools in our league was a humbling experience. It not only hurt; it made me mad.

But status is relative. Yes, compared to the schools in our athletic league, Rivers, in many respects, was the bottom-feeder. The school paled as well in comparison to schools outside the ISL, like Concord Academy or Winsor. There were other schools outside the ISL that the school competed with in admissions. Some were considered progressive. Others focused on learning issues, and still others emphasized personal attention. None of these schools had strong reputations for excellence. Rivers won many of the common admits with these schools while losing students to the ISL schools. Clearly, the school was trying to straddle two market segments — never a good strategy.

In addition to the rationalizations for underperformance, some community members advanced their own solutions to rectify the school's lowly status, often after they remarked on how caring the school was. Of course, the best was upgrading the dress code. The logic went something like this: if our students looked more like those at a local traditional boys' school, they might perform better — more status by association.

In fact, status by association was a major driver in parents' decisions to send their children to Rivers. After all, the school was in the prestigious ISL and had a typical college prep program. The occasional stories of excellence gave the communications department just enough material to indulge parents' fantasies that Rivers was part of the "club." If the school played Groton, surely Rivers and Groton had something in common beyond athletics. In the absence of a purpose for seventy years, Rivers let the market define it, and it happily accommodated those definitions, at least the occasional positive ones.

A SWOT analysis should not focus only on weaknesses. Rivers had some key strengths that could be leveraged to launch a change effort. First, although the school was the doormat of the ISL, it was in a league of schools that had strong academic and athletic reputations. As a result, there was a significant opportunity to strengthen the school's brand by being competitive in this prestigious league. In the late 1990s and early 2000s, the Boston high school athletic scene was different from any I had ever seen. Except for football, the independent schools were seen as the athletic powerhouses. Independent schools in this area of the country recruited athletes heavily. This led to better teams. In addition, these schools realized that the most elite colleges gave extra consideration to strong athletes in the admission process. If the student-athlete falls within the Ivy Index and the college coach wants that student, the student is often admitted. This practice extended to the prestigious small colleges in the Northeast as well. Recruit some solid students who were outstanding athletes, and a prep school can burnish the college list, which can lead to more academically talented students applying to the school. In the world of selective admissions in the Northeast, the A+ student with scores of 5 on ten AP Exams was no match for the B student who weighed 250 pounds and could tackle with the best of them. No asterisk was placed next to the name of a recruited athlete on the school's college list.

For me, college matriculation to highly selective colleges was always a means to an end. In the realm of academics, I wanted an intellectually vibrant school in which ideas flowed freely, and student engagement was the norm. Attracting a significant percentage of intellectually curious students was necessary to establish this climate. In the Boston independent school world, this would only happen if some percentage of students enrolled in highly selective colleges. If athletic excellence provided a pathway to achieve this goal, I was more than happy to take it.

Second, the Rivers Music School, owned by The Rivers School but mostly independent of it, had developed an outstanding reputation as one of the best music schools in the area. It could not be compared to the New England Conservatory, but several of its part-time teachers also taught at NEC. The music school had grown rapidly in the 80s and 90s, and the vast majority of its students did not attend The Rivers School, mostly viewing the school as weak and not worth the tuition. But each week, about 500 mostly very bright and talented student musicians came to the Rivers campus because of the quality of music instruction. All those talented, smart kids on our campus — this had to be a huge opportunity for the school.

Third, Rivers was blessed to have a talented and frugal CFO who counted every penny, managed budgets that frequently led to surpluses, and protected the school's money as if it were his own. After his email signature, in Latin, were the words, "Money does not grow on trees." Over the years, his vigilant oversight of the budget led to an accumulated surplus of $2 million. It took me an exasperating two months to pry this information out of him, but in the end, I was grateful for his frugality.

Fourth, there were several outstanding teachers at the school, outstanding by any measure. They were challenging and engaging. They communicated to students that although the standards were high, they wanted the students to succeed but not by compromising those standards. Everybody in the school knew who they were, and they proved to be exemplars for the kind of teaching I wanted to see across all departments.

Fifth, Boston was a Mecca for talent. There were successful entrepreneurs, business consultants, and executives who could bring a wealth of knowledge to the boardroom. Long a hub for education, Boston provided a plethora of outstanding teachers as well. And money was being made hand over fist in the 1990s. Despite the intense competition, it was hard to imagine a better place to dramatically improve an independent school.

My obsession with attracting and keeping talent, especially teachers, stemmed from my work with Rod Snelling, the founder of Independent School Management. Early in my career, as we prepared to establish a new Episcopal high school in southwest Louisiana, the initiative's leaders hired Rod to provide consulting. In my late 20s, having already joined the administrative ranks, I had the privilege of learning from this data-driven independent school guru. Subsequently, I came to disagree with Rod on some of his approaches to management, but his fervent belief that the foundation for a thriving independent school begins with great teachers continues to drive my thinking about the critical elements in establishing a foundation for positive change. A school leader can have the greatest ideas imaginable, but if she cannot attract talent, those ideas will only remain dreams.

Sixth, there existed a palpable bond between students and teachers. Although, at times, strong teacher relationships with students seemed to be an easy, no-cost way of disguising mediocrity in the classroom, Rivers had a genuine culture of caring and a desire to treat each other with kindness and respect. I have no doubt that this culture originated in the early years of the school and survived despite the vicissitudes of the school's history.

Seventh, the fine arts department at Rivers was strong in both the middle and upper schools. I was astounded by some of the student art work and the dedication of the teachers. In 1997, it was unclear how I could leverage this gem. I did not see it as a principal driver in the marketplace, but it could become a strong secondary reason for talented students to enroll.

So, strengths and opportunities, two key elements in a SWOT analysis, seemed to blend in ways that, with a little imagination and some dot-connecting, could lead to establishing a real strategy.

You might be asking now about the "threats" part of the SWOT. In analyzing other schools, I take "threats" seriously, especially for well-established schools that can easily fall prey to complacency. But in 1997, as I was learning about Rivers and thinking about possibilities, I paid little attention to the "T" part of the SWOT. I knew the cards were stacked against us; defense was not an option. Moreover, I was emboldened by the possibility of finally calling the question after seventy years of wandering in the darkness. I knew there would be risks, but I liked the challenge. In retrospect, there were a few times when I regretted the decision to ignore threats. We may have been better prepared for the unintended consequences of paths taken, and yes, there were many. But in the end, my sense of urgency to awaken the school from its seventy-year slumber prevailed. Full-steam ahead.

Questions

1. What is your plan and timeline for developing a deep understanding of the school?

2. What is your plan for building relationships with key stakeholder groups?

3. What data must be analyzed? What story does it tell?

4. What are the prevailing narratives in the school? Will they help or hinder change efforts?

5. What elements of the school's history might be used as a justification for change?

6. What is the school's current reputation in the community? How do you know?

7. As you conduct the SWOT and begin to formulate theories, with whom can you discuss your preliminary thoughts?

8. The presentation of your SWOT to the board and faculty will be one of the most important during your tenure. How will you prepare? Who will give you honest feedback?

9. What are the threats that may need to be addressed as part of your strategy? What local and national trends might be relevant?

Reader's Notes

Chapter 4

Vision: "A Winning Aspiration"

In *Playing to Win*, the first question, "What is your winning aspiration?" captures both the practical and the idealistic. For any organization to add value, it needs to have a North Star. But that North Star cannot simply be whatever the CEO values the most. The goal has to be achievable, and it has to be devised with a pragmatic eye on the organization's capabilities, market conditions, and assets, both human and other. In addition, according to Martin and Lafley, organizations that want sustainable change cannot simply strive for competitiveness; they must strive to win. They need to examine the market not just with the imagination of an artist but also with a cold calculus that accounts for the industry, the customer, the product, and more. In addition, they argue that striving to win, as opposed to just competing, leads stakeholders to take the goals seriously and allocate the proper resources, time, energy, and money to achieve them. This means that a school can't just dip its toe in the water. It has to make a commitment, a full investment in achieving its vision. Absent this commitment, the easy default is to create a hodge-podge of initiatives, hoping the school can be all things to everyone.

Heads of school struggle with the "vision thing" often because they don't understand what it is or how it pertains to leading an independent school. Most new heads just want to go about the business of making their mark on the school. This attitude is understandable but limited in its capacity to unleash the creativity of others. If told to create a vision, many heads, I suspect, would not know where to begin. It's easy to understand why.

The truth is that creating a vision is hard; it requires self-knowledge, imagination, an understanding of the landscape of reality, and a rigorous commitment to the school's mission. It is much easier to be a chief problem-solver.

Of these key leadership qualities, the one most visibly absent is imagination. I have encountered a lot of very intelligent heads during my career, but many of them lack imagination. It's as if their left-brain dials are turned to 10, and their right brains are in sleep mode. These kinds of leaders gravitate to the problem-solving mode. Independent school leaders must understand that a critical component of real strategy is imagination, a quality we all have but often don't use.

In my experience, many heads simply bypass the creation of a "winning aspiration." Perhaps they don't know where to start, so they ignore the question. I suspect they gravitate to easier, more palatable approaches and count them as visions. For some, vision is simply what was successful at their former schools: "If it worked at School X, it's bound to work here." This shallow thinking often results in the establishment of random programs, lacking a common theme. It also disregards the specific circumstances of the new school. Vision can also go awry when the head fails to reign in her passions, disregarding the school's mission, its culture, its history, and the marketing realities it faces. It's as if the head is determined to inflict her educational passions on the school regardless of its circumstances. It's a subtle form of hubris.

A powerful vision comes from the head's knowledge of herself and her passions, the nature of the market, the history, mission, and values of the school, and the resources available to achieve the dream. Creating a vision is the head's responsibility, not the responsibility of the trustees. There is no way that trustees have the time or the expertise to gain the kind of deep insights into a school that will become the foundation of a vision. However, trustees do need to stress test the head's vision. They must question and probe:

1. Will the realized vision advance the mission?
2. Will the market respond to the vision if achieved?
3. Does the school have the capabilities to achieve the vision?
4. Can the vision inspire stakeholders?

Creating a vision begins with the head's self-knowledge, the true drivers of her actions, and what she is most passionate about in education. To be sure, the head's passion alone is an insufficient justification for a vision. However, if it can combine with the practical elements of a "winning aspiration," this passion can inspire stakeholders to achieve spectacular results. The head's passion animates the vision; it speaks to the stakeholders' emotions. Therein lies its power. And unlike the for-profit world, the leader's passion points to a greater cause and the possibility of adding meaning to the lives of stakeholders. Passion is essential to a head's vision; without it, there is little possibility of creating a community in service to building something great. In the school business, the head can constantly reference the vision to remind trustees, faculty, and administrators why their work matters and how it is making a difference in the lives of young people. (Olverson, June 2015, RG 175 Blog)

A compelling vision is also one that makes sense. It's part of the school's larger historical narrative, creating a thread from past to present to future. It allows the head to draw on the past to demonstrate to stakeholders that a revolution is not being born. Rather, the school is honoring its history. Van Wyck Brooks, the literary critic, coined the phrase "usable past." The term is apt for any major change effort in independent schools. It suggests that heads study the school's history and look for those threads that can be pulled forward and projected into the future to develop consensus and maintain continuity.

Even as Rivers languished for seventy years, in its history were pockets of real success, real excellence. Most notably, the school moved to its permanent home in Weston, a monumental undertaking that opened up new possibilities for future leaders. In addition, the school successfully transitioned to co-education. There were also faculty heroes who transformed students' lives in so many ways. More specifically, in the 1970s, when Rivers was still all-boys, it had an excellent athletic program. There were numerous championship banners from that era hanging in the gym. Thus, the focus on athletic excellence after I became head was merely a replay of the success the school enjoyed in an earlier era.

As I justified the school's changes, I could point to these significant successes to convince stakeholders that I wasn't trying to pull a rabbit out of a hat but rather demonstrate that excellence had always been a part of Rivers' past.

To be clear, Rivers failure was not to invest in *sustaining excellence.* Yet its successes were part of a foundation for future sustainable change because they captured the narrative of excellence in the school's history. The failure to sustain excellence points to an important lesson for school leaders. Sustainable change only comes about when a school is playing the long game, when its leaders are thinking about systems, structures, and culture as vehicles for on-going improvement now and into the future.

As mentioned earlier, many veteran heads and consultants advise new heads to take several months at the beginning of their tenures to learn about the school, its programs and its culture. But what is rarely mentioned is the connection between learning about the school and developing a vision. The deep insights gained from studying the school's history, culture, and mission, interviewing veteran faculty and administrators, and talking with trustees and former trustees become the foundation for change. This deep learning sets the stage for the head to use her imagination to integrate her deeply held beliefs about education, the challenges and opportunities the school faces, the school's potential in the market, and its capabilities in executing a plan.

There's no straight-line path when it comes to using your imagination to develop a vision for the school; a head must simply do a lot of thinking in the belief that her creative self will kick in. I once heard Peter Senge, the M.I.T. systems guru back in the 1990s, tell an audience: "If you are trying to get a plant to grow, you don't stand over it and yell, "Grow, damn it, grow! You prepare the soil, get rid of the weeds, water the ground, and more." The same is true with vision. You listen, you study, you learn, you think, you hope, and you wait.

The power of a well-conceived, realizable vision is that it not only has the power to solve many of the weaknesses in the SWOT analysis but also unleashes the creativity and commitment of others. Such creativity leads to results far exceeding solutions to discrete problems.

In implementing the strategic plan at Rivers, initially, I had seven to ten ideas or general directions for improvement. Most of these ideas were not programmatic in nature; they were structural. After the first four years, my role as chief architect of strategic initiatives diminished. Fresh ideas came from faculty and staff. As a result, I focused on two tasks: 1) make sure that smaller visions, coming from faculty and administrators, supported the bigger vision and 2) move boulders out of the way so these bright, creative people could add value to the school.

Of course, clearing the pathway, as opposed to being the originator of all initiatives, implies that a leader has enough humility to let others shine. This is a key element of leadership. Effective leaders are not intimidated by talent; they embrace and cultivate it. Their humility reflects their self-confidence and their deep desire for their organization to win. Humility does not suggest that the leader is indecisive. It means that she is constantly open to learning and sharing. She knows that the very success of the organization depends on creating the conditions that allow talent to work its miracles.

"My goal is to be the dumbest guy in this room, and I'm pretty smart," said the Rivers math department chair while he was C.E.O. of one of his start-ups. At first, it seemed an odd statement. Shouldn't the C.E.O. be the most knowledgeable person in the room? Shouldn't the leader have all the answers and know what to do and when to do it? The questions illuminate our preconceptions of leadership that are outdated and useless. Yet, they persist, and their pernicious impact prevents schools from tapping the latent talent and wisdom within the community.

What was behind the math department chair's statement? What are the assumptions about leadership, and what might a head of school glean from them?

The first assumption is an unwavering commitment to talent. The head of school might be the smartest person in the room, but with a void of talent around her, the school will flounder or, at the very least, fail to reach its potential. Talent touches the quality of everything a school does. Attracting and retaining talent to optimize the school's performance is one of the most critical jobs of a head of school. True leaders are never intimidated by talent.

The second assumption is a belief in the collective wisdom of a group. Good management is partly about using conversation and collaboration to frame the right questions to find the best answers. One head of school often told his senior administrative team, "Best idea wins." It makes no difference where great ideas come from; what matters is that they are great. True leaders know this and create conditions that encourage talented players to have a strong voice in the team's deliberations.

The third assumption is that learning never stops. When a head makes it clear that she can learn from senior administrators and expects to learn from them, she is unleashing the most powerful tool any organization has – the expertise and creativity of its employees. Learners do not care from whom they learn. They just want to gain profound insights into the landscape of reality in order to optimize the school's efforts. Introducing new information, challenging assumptions, reframing issues, analyzing data, and recognizing biases are all critical in making good decisions. They are examples of real learning. And they lie dormant when heads of school lack the self-confidence to be wrong.

The fourth assumption is that the head of school's self-confidence sets the stage for success by focusing on winning instead of playing political games. Effective leaders do not need their egos constantly stroked. Nor do they create soap operas that confer more status on one or more of the senior leaders, ultimately pitting one against another. In eschewing the need for her ego to be massaged, the real leader demonstrates the strength of humility to help the organization win by maximizing its collective talent.

A striking example of the benefits of providing space for others to shine came from the middle school head I hired for the 1998-99 school year. One of the strategic goals was to create a dynamic, cutting-edge middle school that prepared students for the upper school. To be honest, I wasn't sure what "cutting edge" really looked like, but intuitively, I knew that the middle school program when I arrived was not meeting the needs of this age group.

In 1997, the Rivers middle school consisted of grades 7 and 8. It had 62 students, and several teachers straddled between the middle and upper schools. It looked like a typical junior high school but much smaller. Clearly, this division needed new leadership.

The selection of a new middle school head came down to two finalists. The first was an experienced administrator from New Jersey who was, at the time, a middle school head. The second was an 8th grade English teacher from Ohio who had no administrative experience but possessed a deep passion for the education of this age group. Backsliding into my cautious mode, I offered the job to the experienced candidate. She eventually turned it down; to this day, I am grateful she did. It was yet another example of the role luck can play in one's success. I value experience, but I am much more drawn to a learner with passion. In this instance, I betrayed that value but did not suffer the consequences.

After a rocky start, the inexperienced new middle school head, a truly gifted educator, transformed a sleepy junior high school into one of the most innovative middle schools in the area. A sixth grade was added, enrollment doubled, grading was eliminated by 2004, and multi-grade advisory groups were created in order to mitigate the social problems that define so many middle schools. Parents were dazzled by conferences with all their child's teachers at the same time and in the same room. Under the new leadership, humanity (a key word in the eventual Rivers' vision) was no longer merely a proxy for caring and compassion; it was a driving principle that informed every aspect of the middle school program. To educate this age group, teachers needed to understand the developmental stages, both intellectual and emotional, these children were going through. They could no longer separate the academic and the non-academic in educating their students. I once asked the middle school head about a teacher "wasting" precious class time on a social issue. She replied, "Tom, if you don't think what happens to a 13-year-old during the break impacts her learning in the classroom, you do not understand this age group." Lesson learned.

The middle school head did not just take me to the edge; she dangled me over the cliff. Given the changes these children were undergoing, she had a clear vision of what middle school education should look like, and she was going to find expression for her deepest creative impulses. Implicitly, she drove the entire school to think expansively about "Excellence with Humanity." These words ultimately became the vision for the school. She forced us to de-compartmentalize the lives of adolescents and fill our vision with new possibilities. Through their dedication, she and the middle school faculty created story after story that I could use to illustrate what Rivers was all about. Combined with the more traditional measures of excellence soon to come in the upper school, the story machine started to hum.

A vision should not be didactic and rigid with a set of principles that dictate actions in a lockstep manner. Crossing off a list of items without considering results is a waste of time. Instead, a vision should invite creativity and thus, re-definition. Once Rivers had settled on "Excellence with Humanity," my definition changed three times over the course of the next twelve years because teacher creativity forced me to re-think its major tenets. Faculty used their imaginations, I watched and listened, and I repeatedly returned to the drawing board: What does "Excellence with Humanity" really mean?

The success of the middle school program at Rivers was due, in large part, to its comprehensiveness; the middle school philosophy touched every aspect of the student experience. This approach was very different from the add-on courses or programs that schools develop in hopes of changing their status in the marketplace. In recent years, I have talked with several heads who see programmatic changes, in and of themselves, as essentially a vision. The programmatic changes derive from the desire to offer something distinctive in comparison to the competition.

One school head focused efforts on opportunities for authentic learning in the high school. Juniors and seniors gained agency over their education, designing authentic projects that allowed them to delve into a particular interest. The school touted the introduction of this graduation requirement as a reflection of its forward-thinking approach to education. There were a handful of stories in the other divisions about students "owning" their learning. The school had suffered enrollment declines for the past twenty-five years and had dipped into its endowment for financial aid to prop up the size of the school. It decided to implement this new curriculum, emphasizing student autonomy as the differentiator that would drive students to the school. It failed.

Program changes, at least those that seem like gestures, are implementation steps; they are not a vision. Too many schools chase the hottest trend in independent school education, thinking it can solve their enrollment problems. Creating a vision that strengthens or substantially modifies a school's brand requires research and deep thinking, the results of which must be applied across departments. For Rivers, that meant asking the question, "What does "Excellence with Humanity" mean in college counseling, school culture, fundraising, admissions, teaching standards, and more?" Once the school answered these questions and executed the resulting plans, word-of-mouth had the potential to become more than talk about a single program. The school gave parents the words to use, and their students' experiences in multiple arenas gave them examples.

With schools that suffer from an identity crisis, I ask the head to conduct an exercise with the trustees and the faculty to encourage their thinking about what they want and what they think potential parents want:

> *Imagine that a parent from your school is asked, "Tell me about your child's experience at School X; what stands out?" In ten years, what do you want 70% of your parents to say are the three most distinguishing features of the school?*

For a school to build a powerful brand that will drive behavior and overcome the barrier of high tuition, it has to create multiple student experiences that lead to top-of-mind attributes that students and parents come to value. These valued attributes lead to the Holy Grail of marketing - positive word-of-mouth. A capstone project and the elimination of AP classes are insufficient, in and of themselves, to drive behavior in the marketplace. There may be good reasons to take these actions, but a head should not think that these efforts will solve a school's enrollment problems or establish a brand that will drive prospective families to the school.

Furthermore, independent schools, staking their future on a program, can often become intoxicated by their own ideas because they are not using a customer lens. The insularity in these schools makes it easy for them to fall in love with their initiatives without stress-testing them.

To be clear, I would admire a school that sacrifices enrollment in order to fulfill a mission that the stakeholders powerfully feel. If there is a passion for a particular approach to teaching and learning (Montessori, for instance), then fully commit to it, knowing that your enrollment may drop. However, program changes are not a vision. Having a capstone project in the junior and senior years and some student choices about what science topic will be studied in third grade are not compelling in the marketplace. Strategy requires bigger thinking. If enrollment matters, consider the customers and remember that differentiators are not magic bullets. For differentiators to work, they have to be compelling.

If creating a vision sounds squishy, I understand. I wish I could give you an easy how-to manual with step-by-step directions, eventually leading to the perfect vision for your school. But you can't create a great vision painting by numbers. Vision requires creativity and patience. Expecting the answer at the beginning of your journey is not going to work. You have to ruminate on what you are passionate about, what you have learned about the school, and what the market will embrace. Look for the intersections, those places that reflect the school's mission, its values, and the need to win in the marketplace. Think and dream. Use trial and error. The marketing committee meetings led by the Monitor consultant often made my brain tired as he kept asking deeper and more thoughtful questions. A head should feel this when she is doing serious work to develop a vision.

Facing that complexity head-on, though, can eventually lead to something special. The right vision creates a community of shared meaning in which stakeholders can be part of creating something bigger and greater than any individual. In particular, faculty and administrators are able to use their creativity to build programs that will help realize the vision and fulfill their professional and creative aspirations. The head can use the vision to rally the stakeholders and inspire them to see their work as more than just a job but rather as a life purpose. Just as importantly, vision begins to establish guardrails, which act as critical management tools to keep stakeholders focused.

Vision is the foundation of leadership. In fact, a school with a clear, well-articulated vision may not need a formal and structured strategic plan with priorities and timelines. Generating enthusiastic buy-in will align behavior with a clear purpose in achieving the vision. It ensures clarity about what the school is and what it is not. Everybody in the school knows where it is headed and why.

One needs to look no further than Harvard-Westlake School in Los Angeles, one of the premiere co-educational day schools in the country, and its stunning success over the last thirty years to realize that strategic plans are not always necessary. With an extraordinarily talented faculty and staff, Harvard-Westlake was inspired by its founding president Tom Hudnut. Tom's vision was clear, concise, and compelling: Harvard-Westlake will have a faculty worthy of its outstanding student body and a student body worthy of its distinguished faculty. In partnership with his board chair, a Stanford alumna, he took his vision one step further: Harvard-Westlake will be the day-school equivalent of Stanford University. It would be a school with excellent programs across the board. No strategic plan needed!

My background made it easy to reflect on what excited me about independent school education. It was all about excellence and relationships, and it was rooted in my independent school experience. I was accepted to St. Stephen's Episcopal School in Alexandria, Virginia, for my junior year. The Academic Dean indicated that I could take Honors Pre-calculus if I took Honors Algebra II in summer school. The summer class produced a moment I still remember fifty-four years later. At my old school I was accustomed to math tests that essentially consisted of problems quite similar to the homework problems. In other words, the problems were the same, just different numbers. If you memorize the process, you could usually make an A. When I took my first summer school math test at St. Stephen's, I saw several problems I had never seen before. I was certain there was a mistake, so I went to the teacher's desk and politely said, "Excuse me, sir. I think there is a mistake. There are a number of problems on the test that we never reviewed." He looked at me quizzically for a moment and said, "So?" I returned to my desk. I think I made a D on the test. But I learned a lesson.

A candidate for a head position told me in an interview: "The purpose of most independent schools should be to teach students how to do hard things well." The statement captured the value of my St. Stephen's education. I learned how to face academic challenges. It energized me. I loved the intellectual challenge and the chance to figure things out, make connections, and draw conclusions. I wanted Rivers students to strive for excellence and love the striving.

The emphasis on relationships in the development of a vision was a no-brainer. Throughout my career, I saw the profound difference teachers had on students as they went the extra mile to connect with them, pat them on the back, or tell them a hard truth. Despite seeing it firsthand, I thought schools did an abysmal job demonstrating this attribute to parents. Independent schools tout small classes and an advisor program as proxies for knowing and understanding students. I wanted to see if Rivers could move beyond this formulaic pitch to create structures that showed parents that our knowledge of their children was at a whole new level. I saw this as a huge marketing opportunity once the school had joined the constellation of good and great schools. My math department chair/entrepreneur once told me, "Tom, if you want me to be a repeat customer, deliver on your promise. If you want me to spread the word, dazzle me." Small class sizes and an advisor system seemed stale. My team saw bigger possibilities.

In using the term "winning aspiration," Martin and Lafley are quite clear about the need to create a vision that can be achieved. The authors also clearly state that the objective is to win the market space, not just compete. In 1997-98, I struggled with finding the right wording for a vision. I intuitively understood that Rivers needed to be the best at something. I knew that the "something" needed to combine excellence with caring per my educational passions, the history of the school, and the context of a competitive independent school market. I also believed that lots of parents valued both excellence and caring and indeed, this belief was substantiated with data when Rivers conducted a brand study several years later. In addition, my team knew that Rivers could not produce the results associated with the highest level of academic excellence. It was not going to have a college list comparable to that of Roxbury Latin, a school known for the highest standards of academic excellence. Using traditional measures, Rivers was not going to "out-excellence" the elite.

Although we clearly understood how excellence and caring could work together to create a compelling case, we felt stuck. From a marketing perspective, excellence was a table stakes. In other words, Rivers would need a certain level of academic, athletic and artistic excellence to compete with the other ISL schools. Caring was the attribute that could distinguish the school, not because it was absent at the other schools, but rather because these schools were inconsistent in demonstrating how well they knew the students.

I also had learned from my research that in many of the highly-regarded schools, there was a cut-throat culture and an academic intensity that, for some of their students, led to an unhappy experience — conditions that created opportunities for a school like Rivers.

Caring did not capture the entirety of the differentiator we had in mind. It was too narrow. Furthermore, the connotation of the word raised a red flag. Does caring imply "excellent lite?" "Excellence with Caring" felt like an invitation to maintain the status quo, enabling the school community to feel better about itself without really changing. If we used the word "balance," we faced the same dilemma.

For the next three to four years, we struggled with the wording of the vision. It was a perfect example of how difficult it is to create a vision that says exactly what the school intends. It's not difficult for a new head to come into a very good school and see that the facilities need to be improved and from that observation, create a vision: "School X will have facilities that match the quality of its programs."

But when a school is attempting to establish or strengthen an identity and use strategy to do so, words matter. They matter to faculty and staff looking for behavioral cues in this new order; they matter to other stakeholders who need to understand the direction of the school. Without some succinct articulation of a vision that connected excellence with caring, what's left was the goal of becoming one of many good independent schools in the Boston area. Because of my quietly competitive nature, I refused to let Rivers simply strive to be yet another good independent school in a very crowded market of good independent schools. Either a business makes a better mouse trap than all the other mouse trap manufacturers or it creates a whole new category and wins there. I was after the former. To me, the pathway to winning was uniting excellence and caring. We just could not find the right words.

In retrospect, we probably worried about this conundrum too much. The Herculean task of establishing a reputation of excellence consumed most of our time and energy in those first years anyway.

In the early 2000s, luck found me yet again.

Our admissions office had decided to do a substantial upgrade of the viewbook. The director of admissions settled on a firm with some imaginative and keenly insightful designers. They spent hours on the campus, walking around and interviewing students, teachers, and administrators. Even though we hadn't articulated the vision, the designers figured out what the school was trying to achieve. The lead designer wanted a title for the new viewbook, and he came up with "Excellence with Humanity." The members of the administrative team were intrigued. They saw that "humanity" was more expansive than "caring," and it did not carry the baggage that "caring" did. It was abstract enough that it gave the school room to provide its own definition and grow into the possibilities. After a while, we were sold. Rivers would be the best school in the Boston area for combining excellence with humanity. Twenty years later, "Excellence with Humanity" remains the tagline for the school and the short form of its purpose.

At Rivers, we created a vision that was designed to substantially clarify the school's identity. And to be sure, a vision needs to speak to a school's existing or desired market position. But it does not always have to shoulder the full responsibility of establishing a market identity. A vision might focus on facilities, stakeholder engagement, community, character, or the student/faculty experience. The critical point is that the expression of the vision successfully touches multiple areas of the school so that the school's identity is strengthened.

At Rivers, the deep thinking required to develop a "winning aspiration" eventually provided a clear path forward. The job was straight-forward: 1) make excellence a stronger part of the school's identity so that it was clearly a part of the constellation of good and great schools in the Boston area, and 2) once a part of this constellation of schools, distinguish the school through culture and programs that reflect the school's commitment to humanity. We still knew that we were playing a game that we could lose, but now we had distilled our ideas so that we could see a pathway to action.

ıestions

1. When in your weekly schedule will you set aside time to think about the school's strategic direction?

2. What potential vision are you most passionate about? What are the distinguishing features of your ideal school?

3. Does your vision call on the school's past to propel it forward?

4. Is your vision succinct? Can it be applied to all parts of the school's operation?

5. Will your vision win in the market? If realized, is it compelling? How do you know?

6. In ten years, what do you want parents to say are the three top-of-mind qualities of the school? How are those qualities distinctive and compelling in comparison to those of other schools?

7. Who will you use to help stress-test your vision before presenting it to the board and faculty?

8. What steps must you take to build consensus for the proposed direction of the school? Which influencers might need special attention?

<u>Reader's Notes</u>

Chapter 5

Strategy with the Customer in Mind

The story has become all too familiar. The economy slides, enrollment drops, and the school needs to meet the budget numbers. Switching to reactive mode, leadership starts taking students who are not mission-appropriate. The downward spiral is launched.

Another school throws a lot of ideas to increase enrollment against the proverbial wall to see which ones stick. "If we offer several mediocre product lines, maybe we will get more customers," the misguided thinking goes.

So many independent schools follow these brand-killing strategies, and after several years, even the short-term gains become long-term headaches. Teachers and administrators start asking, "Who are we?" It's sad to encounter these schools. Faculty morale is often low because teachers bear the brunt of a school without a clear purpose.

I interviewed teachers at one school that suffered from an identity crisis, in this case, a failure to clarify the types of students it could best serve. Dedicated professionals were worn out with trying to serve so many different student needs. Administrators made it clear that they wanted high scores on the AP Exams and at the same time, "caved" to parents who demanded that their unqualified students be allowed to take AP courses. They were fearful of losing the students. In addition, teachers needed to stay in touch with the tutoring center about the progress, or lack thereof, of these students. In a perfect illustration of the impact of misalignment, the school did not charge extra for the many students who used the learning center. So, at the same time that the school pushed teachers to attain high AP scores, it incentivized families whose children needed significant extra help, leading to more and more of these families coming to the school. Instead of developing a realistic strategy to thrive, the school scrambled to maintain enrollment and all the baggage that comes with this mindset. I raised the issue with the trustees. They listened, nodded politely, and then proceeded to another issue.

The above example reveals the pitfalls that come when school leadership fears making a choice or fails to even comprehend the need to make a choice. Trying to win in two different market segments is a fool's errand. It leads to the triumph of the short term over the long term, the failure to properly allocate time, energy, and money to solidify a market position, and a prescription for death by a thousand cuts. "How's enrollment looking this year?" The question dominates the narrative within the school community and thus, reinforces a mindset that focuses on the short term. (Olverson, March 2019, RG 175 Blog)

When the demographics and local economy are favorable, it's easy for a school to become complacent about its identity. Afterall, enrollment is strong, and the school is recording surpluses. Trustees laud the head and the director of admissions for their excellent work.

But for too many schools, strong enrollment disguises the failure of the school to capture a market position, which, in turn, makes it subject to the future whims of the market and the emerging demographics. At some point, the economy will falter, and enrollment will drop. The weakness of the value proposition is laid bare, often resulting in finger-pointing or "learned helplessness" to use Martin Seligman's term.

Because schools that lack clarity in the marketplace often don't want to address the real issue, they come up with a litany of superficial reasons for declining enrollment or lower numbers of applications:

"We need to do a better job of spreading the word."

"We need a new director of marketing and communications."

"Our website needs to be better."

"We need to look more like the schools beating us in the market."

"We're the best-kept secret in town."

"We need a better athletic program."

"We need a new head."

The contortions these schools put themselves through can be astounding. They will do anything to avoid holding up a mirror and telling the truth. I understand the reluctance of trustees to tackle big questions like which market segment it wants to compete in and therefore, what kinds of students it wants to attract. It requires making a choice and the inevitable pain that comes with making that choice. Is it really plausible to think that trustees will alienate friends in the community by choosing a path for the school that does not align with their friends' perceived needs or maybe even their own needs? Is it plausible that they will sacrifice their short-term interests for the long-term health of the school.

Here's where the practical realities collide with the platitudes in so many "How to Govern" manuals. Most trustees will not alienate friends, business partners, or high-profiled community leaders to make the choices necessary to establish or strengthen the school's market niche. When schools avoid the essential choices that arise from developing a strategy, there are often other agendas driving decision-making, some of which may have nothing to do with the school or its challenges.

Only the leadership of the head can overcome the significant headwinds preventing the school from changing. By forcing the board to abandon its parochial concerns and instead, think strategically, the head can establish the foundation for sustainable change. This is a difficult and time-consuming task in which the head forces the board to focus on the needs of future students by first establishing a consensus about the current reality.

In the independent school world, the answer to the question "Where to play?" is intimately tied to the aspirational identity of the school. The aspirational identity springs from the school's mission, but even a clear mission is simply not sufficient to guarantee the school's sustainability. Leadership has to determine the market segment it wants to play in, the school's competition, the kinds of students it is trying to attract, and the distinguishing elements that will be compelling differentiators. In short, who are the customers the school is targeting? What are their values? Where do they live? What will attract them to the school? The answers to these questions are essential in determining strategy.

But even schools with clear identities in the market must never let their guards down. Protecting the school's reputation and understanding the potential threats against it are two of the most critical responsibilities of the head and the board of trustees. This responsibility includes constantly looking for ways to solidify the school's identity while ensuring the mission is being lived. Will the goals of a strategic plan strengthen the school's market position, or will they weaken it? Will they clarify or obscure?

In conversation with a high-level executive at a global company, I learned the extent to which a successful business will go to protect its brand. Junior executives were constantly presenting alternate opportunities for the company to enhance revenue. But the senior executive, leading the team, more often than not, dismissed the ideas. He was worried about compromising the brand of the company. Understanding the importance of protecting the company's market position, he eschewed the opportunities to make money in the short term for fear of the long-term consequences.

Obviously, a corporation like Procter & Gamble has the resources to collect data that will point to plausible answers to questions about the market segment the company wants to compete in. Unfortunately, most independent schools lack these resources and therefore, have to make educated guesses. However, the absence of sophisticated tools to study the market should not prevent an independent school from thinking deeply about the market niche it wants to own, the strategy for capturing it, and ultimately, a realistic assessment of the chances of owning it. Given the absence of data that often leads to greater confidence in decision-making, schools have to speculate and use their best judgment.

As Martin and Lafley demonstrate, answering "Where to play?" requires deep, sophisticated questions. In the previous chapter, I mentioned schools that focused on programmatic changes in a feeble effort to increase enrollment. The flaw in this thinking is the failure to see the development of program as a means, not an end. A program has to join and align with other programs of the school so that, together, they signal a broad narrative about who the school is and what it values. A school that touts only its senior capstone project as an indicator of its innovative approach to education is looking for a quick fix, not a clear identity. If it wants to be known for innovation, the market needs to see its application in multiple areas so parents and students can easily reference it in conversations in the community. Similarly, schools that tout close relationships must demonstrate this feature in all interactions with students, parents, and alumni. One-offs don't build brands.

In many respects, operating in the Boston area allowed me to assume that excellence would be a compelling driver for many prospective families. There was, indeed, a real risk that the presence of so many outstanding prep schools meant that the market was saturated and that "humanity" would never be given a chance to help Rivers differentiate itself because the school would not earn its way into the club in the first place. After a few months on the job, my observations led me to a different conclusion.

In Boston, there is an obsession with excellent education. People are clever in figuring out ways to find out where others went to college as a way of sizing them up. In addition, the public schools outside of Boston were generally excellent and well-funded. I know there are several major cities in the country where similar attitudes exist, but in Boston, it felt like educational excellence and its markers were simply part of the air folks breathed. So, in some ways, the decision to compete in the constellation of good and great schools was a no-brainer. Joining that group of schools would be a major undertaking; distinguishing Rivers within that group of schools would be even more challenging. But it did not feel at all as if the market were saturated.

In the case of Rivers, we had no illusions about the competition. We studied each potential competitor school carefully, noting their many assets. Using the traditional metrics of college placement, endowment, facilities, diversity, and program, we determined what we needed to achieve to compete. These schools had excellent facilities, superior programs, diverse student populations, and large endowments. Excellence was a distinguishing feature for each of them.

The answer to the question, "Where does Rivers want to play?" naturally flowed from the proposed vision. Except for a few boarding schools over an hour away, we wanted to compete against the remaining schools in the ISL, along with a handful of other nearby schools with strong reputations. We wanted to win as many common admits from these schools as we possibly could.

A few years after Rivers decided which schools it wanted to compete against, the Monitor consultant forced us to think more deeply about the market and the profile of those families we were seeking. As we profiled different kinds of customers, he pushed us to think about drivers and barriers. He would ask, "Given this profile, what will drive this family to inquire about Rivers? What will prevent the family from inquiring?"

We discussed issues such as transportation, distance to the school, families with similar values, the number of Rivers families in the same town, perceived prestige, awareness that the school existed, athletics, other programs, and more. We considered all these as we looked for triggers that could move a particular segment to inquire about the school.

Our committee delved into details, and admittedly, there was a lot of speculation without research and data. However, the concept of "drivers and barriers" forced us to take a customer-centric perspective. We began to understand that it's easy for schools to assume that what they value is exactly what the market values. Additionally, the committee began to wrestle with the hard truth that even though the market may be attracted to a particular quality of the school, it may not value it enough to pay a hefty tuition.

I had no illusions about the Herculean task ahead, but the competitive part of my personality wanted to see if "Excellence with Humanity" might begin winning students from some of the elite schools. This raises the issue of the personality of the heads who are leading schools that seek a market niche or desire to strengthen its present niche. Leaders of these schools need to have a competitive streak. When channeled properly, that competitive streak translates into a determination to win and often a belief that "my school's way is better than your school's way." Competitive heads want to prove the superior value of their schools. I know this might sound silly, but knowing the competition and its weaknesses and seeing it as the friendly enemy motivates those in the school community with similar competitive spirits.

Martin and Lafley are quite clear that the answer to the question, "Where will you compete?" must also answer explicitly the question, "Where will you not compete?" The failure of many change efforts in independent schools stems from the unwillingness to confront this critical line of inquiry. There are two principal reasons for asking this question.

First, faculty, staff, trustees, and other stakeholder groups must clearly understand the school's priorities. The renowned business consultant Peter Drucker famously wrote, "The main thing is to make sure that the main thing is the main thing." If a school says that it wants to focus on the individual growth of students, but is still allocating time, energy, and money to the AP program, its words ring hollow, not just with stakeholders but with the market. The program has to produce results that align with the message the school is trying to promote. Misalignment often reflects an absence of clarity about where the school will not compete.

Second, most schools trying to strengthen their market niche lack the resources to invest in multiple priorities. Spreading the investments around various initiatives necessarily means that each of these initiatives will not receive the attention needed to strengthen the brand. Hedging your bets does not work in implementing strategy. Schools have to choose, and the articulation of where the school won't compete diminishes the chances that the school will drift back to the "all things to all people" marketing strategy.

A growing trend in the independent school world is school mergers as a substitute for a marketing strategy. But mergers strike me as a quick fix. In the handful of conversations that I have had with heads about possible mergers, I was struck by the absence of a clear, logical rationale for the move. I heard statements like, "By merging with this elementary school, we'll have the feeder school we need." Or "By merging the two high schools, we'll eliminate the competition." Mergers can easily be viewed as a magic bullet, a simple move that will solve the school's enrollment problems. Martin and Lafley, though, make it quite clear that mergers and acquisitions are not a substitute for strategy. They emphasize that the purpose of strategy is to create value for both the customer and the company. It is difficult to imagine that the mere act of two schools merging creates distinctive value in the marketplace, the one exception being the merger of single-sex schools to become co-ed. But even if a boys' school is merging with a girls' school, if both schools are viewed in the marketplace as mediocre in delivering on their brand promises, then merging, without other major enhancements, will produce little value. Independent schools that stray from the centrality of value-creation in strategic decision-making are necessarily avoiding the most challenging questions but the ones whose answers can yield the most transformative results. Developing strategy is hard work; distrust the simple solutions.

For Rivers, identifying the competition was the easy part of answering the question, "Where do we want to play?" As a consequence of this choice, it would be a monumental task to make excellence a significantly stronger part of the school's identity, but more on that in the next chapter.

Once Rivers had chosen its desired market segment, our marketing efforts focused on the tactical. With no data and no money to gather data, we could not confidently drill down into specific sub-groups to more deeply understand the drivers and barriers to behavior. However, we did theorize that Rivers would have more success attracting students who could create stories of excellence if we concentrated on recruiting students from public schools, at least initially.

The theory was that in the independent elementary schools around the area, top students were predisposed to select a high school with lots of prestige. At most of these schools, Rivers was seen as a "safety." We felt that the perception of the school had calcified to the point that a marketing focus on independent elementary schools would yield little.

Because we suspected their knowledge of independent schools was limited, public school families would more likely lump all the independent schools together — a potential advantage for Rivers. In addition, with public school families, the school could utilize the personal touch, a tactic that often yielded little in the elementary independent school world. All things being equal, with two candidates, one from a public school and one from an independent school, we took the public-school student. We hoped to develop some positive word-of-mouth within those school communities, thus driving more families to Rivers. In addition, although the nearby public schools were generally considered strong, some had average reputations, and could not provide the combination of personal attention and strong academics that the emerging Rivers could. To be sure, there were significant headwinds in our strategy. The volume of students interested in an independent school education was much smaller than one would see at an independent grammar school. In addition, public school families developed strong bonds among themselves and often developed loyalty to their local school system — yet another significant barrier. Despite these headwinds, we reasoned that we would rather play a game with unknowns than one we were almost certain to lose.

Geographically, we focused our attention west of Boston. Rivers is about twelve miles west of downtown Boston. Due west, Rivers had only one competitor from the ISL, and that school was mostly boarding. Because Bostonians place a high value on education, many parents drive their children twenty or more miles to attend a choice school. But still, in the late 90s, traffic in the area was becoming increasingly congested, and with dual-income families, commute time made a difference. In addition, we needed to start winning from Weston, the town where the school is located, and Wellesley, just five minutes away. However, the negative reputation of Rivers was so firmly imbedded in these two towns that it would be ten years before we began to see exploding numbers of applications.

In order for Rivers to establish a foothold in the constellation of good and great schools, it needed more talented students. We were under no illusion that having a superb faculty and coaching staff would magically translate into excellent results. They were necessary but not sufficient. Independent schools cannot simply proclaim their excellence. They have to prove it with results perceived as valuable to targeted families. Rivers needed students with high academic, athletic, and musical potential. It also needed talented students from diverse backgrounds. Enrolling these students was the school's top priority for seventeen years, and it fought the battle on many fronts. We knew these students would not be handed to us on a silver platter; we had to earn them by establishing a great faculty, creating programs that drew them to the school, and finding them in places our competitors might not look.

One of the most important concepts we learned from our Monitor consultant was the necessity of understanding table stakes: what did Rivers need to achieve to be perceived as a true member of the ISL, academically and athletically? In 1997, we lacked the sophisticated and nuanced understanding of table stakes that our Monitor consultant shared with us several years later. However, as stated above, we intuitively understood that if Rivers were to compete confidently against the other ISL schools, it had to produce results.

The study of our potential competitors led to the creation of three strategic goals with specific numerical targets. These goals included placement in the most selective colleges in the country and athletic performance. Two additional goals focused on creating a music program of distinction and a cutting-edge middle school program.

In retrospect, it seems strange to create strategic goals with target numbers. The goals should be broader, the thinking goes, and specific numerical targets should be indicators of success, not success itself. But I wanted the aspirational goals to be clear and results-oriented, especially as I worked with the board of trustees and senior administrators. I was drawn to using numerical targets because they made it difficult to squirm out of the responsibility of achieving the goals. Five years into the plan, I could tell my team and myself, "We've made progress, but we're still not there. What's next?"

Accountability is difficult in independent schools because relationship-building is the very DNA of our schools. But heads can negotiate this dilemma by assuming collective accountability if the team is talented. In other words, the head is not looking for an individual to blame but is asking capable trustees and senior leadership to dig deeper and think harder.

The math department chair, the successful entrepreneur, told his classes on the first day, "Guys, it's not you against me; it's us against advanced algebra." The statement implies exactly the relationship I wanted with the board and senior administrators; I wanted us to hold ourselves accountable, and when we fell short, we would figure it out... together.

When I interviewed Kathy McCartney, the president of Smith College, and asked why she took the job, given the enormous challenges the college faced at the time, her response was illuminating: "I believe in women's education. I know there are challenges. With my team, I'll figure it out." In short, don't play games; don't make excuses. Looking good is not a substitute for being good. Strategic goals with numerical targets made telling the truth about Rivers' performance easier. Collective accountability signaled to us not to become defensive but to work harder and smarter.

Although making choices is crucial in the development of strategy, it is not without pain. When the board and faculty settled on the desired identity of the school, it was my job to communicate this vision to the parents. Many parents were thrilled. The school would raise its academic and athletic standards but not lose its heart.

Others were devastated and angry. One mother, holding back tears, asked, "How can you do this to my child?" About 150 or so parents came to a meeting in which I discussed the new direction for Rivers and then took questions. My presentation was not intended to cast away the many families who had sent their children to Rivers because of the support it offered their students. The school would maintain its commitment to these students. But at the same time, the school would be channeling more resources toward academic excellence and over time, fewer resources to the learning center. More would be expected of students. I did not want to be confrontational, but I did want to be clear. Making a choice was not only necessary, it was also painful.

I think many independent school heads facing identity challenges are unaware of the scale of these challenges. However, I have seen some heads intuit the nature of the challenge and refuse to take it on for fear of the pushback, not to mention the potential loss of enrollment in the short term. Obviously, making these early, often painful, moves requires board support. To the degree that a new head can anticipate the pain of change, she is well served by informing her board of the rough waters ahead. But I suspect that most heads working in underperforming schools don't understand the enormity of the challenge they are facing, and thus, they dabble here and there, add a new center for something or other, or perhaps copy an idea from a school in the region.

The impotence of so many change efforts suggest a key attribute in the leadership of a head-courage. Many of us leaders in the independent school world are people pleasers. We want trustees, parents, faculty, and students to be happy. When a head wants to make bold changes, she must abandon the need to be liked by all. This is not to imply that people skills are unnecessary. EQ is critical in building consensus, navigating the change process, and generating enough enthusiastic buy-in to begin the hard and long journey of adding value to the school. However, heads, beware! The kind of change I am talking about will inevitably make some stakeholders angry.

In my second year at Rivers, a former trustee, an influential political figure in Massachusetts, and a generous benefactor demanded that the school admit a student whose grades and test scores were below average. I refused. We had a meeting that included a current trustee trying to "keep the peace." I would not budge. I am not inflexible. I learned to pay attention to trustees advocating for student applicants and sometimes tried to make it work. But if a head is going to lead a school community in clarifying the school's identity, a line has to be drawn in the sand. A leader cannot establish a new order and then make decisions that align with the old order.

The courage of the head to make difficult decisions indicates her true commitment to building the school's brand. Let me explain what I mean by brand. For many schools, brand is about colors, taglines, web page design, and other outward-facing signs that reflect a consistent message/image about the school. I understand this concept of brand, but my understanding of it goes deeper. For me, brand is a combination of awareness and perspectives of a school, a combination that has the power to drive customer behavior. It's about reputation. Do prospective parents know of the school, do they have favorable or unfavorable attitudes toward it, and to what degree is it top-of-mind for them when they think about independent schools? In addition, there are brand associations. These associations can be linked with performance attributes like 1) excellence, 2) strong academic reputation, 3) strong character development, and 4) personalized attention. But they can also be personal attributes: 1) snobby, 2) friendly, 3) stressful, and 4) traditional. Note that these are customer perceptions, not what senior leadership thinks customer perceptions should be. All of these perceptions are combined to create a picture of the school's ability to drive prospective families to inquire and ultimately, choose it.

When a school has a strong brand, trustees are more likely to focus exclusively on what is best for the school. They are less likely to push personal agendas because the school is bigger than any one individual. It is an honor to serve on the board, and there is no question that the only agenda is fulfilling the school's mission. I am confident this is not the case in all well-established schools, but in general, strong brands keep trustees focused on the issues they should be focused on.

In schools that have weaker brands, the dynamic can be very different. Multiple agendas from trustees can emerge because the weakness of the brand necessarily means a power vacuum. The head's capacity to operate in this vacuum will often determine her success. Citing chapter and verse in a handbook on independent school governance is not going to work. Nor is having the board do a one-day workshop with a consultant. Both assume that trustees joined the board for the sole purpose of making a positive contribution to the school. They just need to be instructed on how to do this.

For schools with weaker brands and, thus, in all likelihood, trustees with other agendas, heads have to know what they are trying to achieve and how they are trying to achieve it. In short, they need to have at least a rough outline of the answers to Martin and Lafley's five questions to use in assessing the agendas of trustees. These answers help heads make good judgments about when to hold the line and when to be flexible. Of course, they need to hold firmly to the mission and values of the school in order to preserve its integrity.

I have heard heads talk with frustration about trustees trying to influence decisions that the heads felt were clearly administrative, as if the line between administration and governance can never be breached. As Rivers strengthened its admission profile, trustees called me frequently to check on the applications of certain students. I paid attention and sometimes negotiated with the admissions office, especially when the trustee was adding value to the school. The critical point here is that heads working for emerging schools need to understand that part of their relationship with some trustees might be transactional and that falling back on a set of rules is a likely prescription for failure. The head should focus on maintaining the school's values and getting to the winner's circle. If a trustee can help with the latter, then the head should look for win-win solutions but never at the expense of achieving or strengthening the desired identity or compromising the school's values.

I delve into the head's judgement to make a critical point: being clear about the vision and goals can make it easier for the head to make the right decisions. But "right" does not mean painless. Schools working toward carving out their positions in the market will most likely have transactional trustees who are willing to toss aside the development of a strong identity in order to get what they want. In these situations, heads will need the courage to remain firm in advocating for the vision. And when the stakes are low, they may need to be flexible. The head's vision and the school's mission and values should inform decision-making.

To ensure that Rivers made a choice about identity and to make sure that I was not the only one walking out on the plank, I took the unusual step of making the trustees vote. Recognizing that achieving consensus at the expense of clarity is easy, I decided that I wanted both. I wrote out four possible profiles of the school, describing the notable features of each one. I reviewed each one with the trustees and answered questions. Then, I made the trustees vote for one. My rationale was that I could not help Rivers become the best Rivers until I knew what Rivers wanted to be. The overwhelming majority voted for the school to make excellence a stronger part of its identity and to distinguish itself by being a caring school. We had yet to come up with the concept of "Excellence with Humanity" at that point, but the trustees understood that caring meant genuine and palpable attention to the many dimensions of each student — intellectual, creative, moral, physical, social, and emotional.

I next turned my attention to the faculty and staff and repeated the exercise. They had more questions than the trustees, many seeing that the old paradigm was truly being threatened. But ultimately, the vast majority voted the same way as the trustees. The votes were a turning point for Rivers. We had our North Star even if we had not yet developed the correct wording. Achieving this consensus also meant I did not have to re-litigate this critical decision. When objections were raised, I could easily reference the vote. It also provided stakeholder groups a context for understanding the school's moves. Priorities emerged, and as a result, not all ideas were equal. The ideas that moved the school closer to realizing the vision moved up the ladder of importance.

Getting a board of trustees to strengthen the school's identity, to include the kinds of students it seeks, is arduous work. Once trustees understand the consequences of making a choice, they may hesitate. But the head and the board chair have to insist that the choice be made. Choosing is essential to strategy. The choice is a key piece to the mosaic because future decisions are now tethered to securing a market segment. The "why" of implementing subsequent change is crystal clear. Many new heads bypass this key choice. But in doing so, they avoid some bumps in the road early in their tenures, but they lose the opportunity to refine the school's purpose, unleash its creativity, and ultimately, strengthen its reputation. For most schools, strategic planning is usually easy because there is nothing strategic about it; choices are avoided. Strategy, on the other hand, is hard.

Racial and socio-economic diversity posed a significant challenge for Rivers. Nearby towns were overwhelmingly white and wealthy. In 1997, the school had less than ten percent students of color. I held out hope for Framingham, which is west of the school and has a significant Latino population. We tried to crack that market but with no success. When the Latino population in Framingham thought of private schools, they thought Catholic. We gave up after a few years of futile attempts to penetrate this market.

Moreover, it was incredibly frustrating to see talented students of color arrive at The Rivers Music School at 4:00 pm after their classes at other schools. Many of them were outstanding academicians as well as excellent musicians. The school would have to earn these students.

The failure to crack the Latino market in Framingham meant that our efforts to recruit students from diverse backgrounds would entail both a wing and a prayer and hand-to-hand combat, one student at a time. To compete against schools with huge endowments and beautiful facilities for students coming out of a prestigious program like Steppingstone (a specialized, tuition-free program that prepares middle school students for prep schools) was going to be difficult. The competition for these excellent students was intense.

ISL schools are bound by league rules not to provide financial aid beyond demonstrated need, a rule that was designed to prevent athletic scholarships. However, rich schools developed their own definitions of demonstrated need while other schools like Rivers used SSS (School and Student Services). The difference in awards could be significant. Rivers was also at a distinct disadvantage in competing for talented students from diverse backgrounds because it lacked the prestige of the other ISL schools. There were no easy answers. Sometimes, it's better to forget about strategy and just dive in, hoping that strategy will find you. We did this in our efforts to recruit students from diverse backgrounds, deciding to learn as we go. Our guide was the associate director of admissions, who found outstanding students from diverse backgrounds by developing relationships with key public-school administrators. Her people skills were off the charts, and the school became more diverse, albeit, at a slower pace than we wished.

It may be tempting for heads and trustees to skip over the question of where the school should compete. Don't. The answer to this question not only helps a school focus on the right customers and what drives their behavior, but also provides important guardrails that can be utilized to prevent rogue characters from pushing the school to stray. Successful strategy is the result of exercising discipline, and that, in turn, takes time. Focusing on the target families forces a school to keep trying to understand them and their motivations. The operating principle is clear; dig deeper, not wider.

Questions

1. What market segment do you want the school to compete in? Why? How does this choice influence your desired results?

2. Will your preferred market segment support your vision?

3. How will you distinguish the school within the desired market segment? Is that distinguishing feature compelling?

4. What are the drivers and barriers to attracting the desired students?

5. How and when will you involve the trustees in choosing a market position? How will you prepare them for the inevitable pushback?

6. What table stakes must be achieved in order to compete in the desired market segment? What proof do you need to provide prospective families?

7. Does your school own a market position? If so, articulate it. How will strategic moves impact that position?

Reader's Notes

Chapter 6

Strategy: How Will You Win?

Although the section in *Playing to Win* on "how" is fascinating, its application to the independent school world is limited. As Martin and Lafley make clear, in the for-profit world, a business generally competes on cost/price or value. If the strategy is cost/price, there is an unrelenting focus on the internal operations to include efficiency and cost-cutting while ensuring quality. If the strategy is value, the focus is external: more and more differentiation from the competitors and obsessive attention on the customers.

Independent schools are people-intensive, making it virtually impossible to find efficiencies that will reduce costs and, thus seemingly precluding a cost strategy. Moreover, the most obvious way to compete in the cost arena is to dramatically increase the size of classes. But for most independent schools, this move cannot be considered because it compromises the essence of the value proposition: strong teacher-student relationships, personal attention, and a school that knows and understands its students as individuals. For the vast majority of independent schools, offering this value is the reason for their existence. Even for schools that compete exclusively against public schools, parents will have some expectation of a minimum standard for a personalized approach to their children's education. Twenty-two students in a class may be fine; thirty is not.

Martin and Lafley make it clear that if a business is going to compete based on cost, it has to have the lowest price to win. Given this principle, if the no-cost option (public school) is seen as good enough, it seems impossible to imagine a scenario in which an independent school could create a financially sustainable model competing on cost. Still, I have often wondered if an independent school in a competitive market might be able to carve out a niche within its chosen constellation of schools by relentlessly focusing on the most critical values of prospective families while ignoring the "prestige" programs that are designed to refine a school's place in the market but which ultimately result in higher tuitions. In the school business, intense competition, counterintuitively, leads to higher tuition. Schools are creating more programs to distinguish themselves; thus, tuition rises. In the Northeast, one need only look at the plethora of specialized centers among many prep schools to understand tuition levels of $50-60,000 for day schools in some markets. Centers focusing on innovation, teaching and learning, civic engagement, entrepreneurship, and STEM can drive up tuition costs unless the school secures funding for the ongoing expenses of these programs.

In contrast, what if a school serving a big city market focused exclusively on a handful of deeply valued attributes that clearly reinforce the desired brand and result in a tuition differential of $15,000 or more? I know some of the specialized centers are designed to help students polish their resumes with compelling extracurricular activities, but might a school tell parents and students that they will need to seek out these extras that speak specifically to their children's interests? Might the lowest cost *within a market segment* drive behavior? In fact, I was recently made aware of The Downtown School in

Seattle, which was spawned from Lakeside School and focuses on excellent teaching but without the myriad of extras that drive tuition in cities like Seattle to absurd levels. Its tuition is a little over $20,000, substantially less than most of the independent schools in the area. MoonshotOS, started by Peter Baron, is rigorously examining the nature of the broken financial model in independent schools and how our industry might address the challenge.

Martin and Lafley's discussion of cost v. value suggests the need to shine an even brighter light on tuition levels in order to arrive at a more nuanced understanding of pricing as it relates to the market. As discussed in a previous chapter, an independent school serving a relatively small population with limited wealth, competing against public schools, has to pay attention to tuition levels. By extension, it must successfully compete in the already established game and not look for new, highly refined categories that put tuition levels out of reach for a significant portion of the population. On the other end of the spectrum, schools serving larger populations with other independent school competitors will need to study and think about the niche they want to own in their respective markets and how that aspiration relates to setting tuition. Notwithstanding the promising innovation of a small cohort of independent schools competing on cost, most big-market schools must continue to think about refining their value proposition as the key driver of market behavior. Big market, small market — every situation is different and requires thoughtful analysis. The Chinese general Sun Tzu advised on strategy: "Know yourself; know your enemy, and know the terrain." The same applies to independent school marketing and pricing. (Olverson, February 2017, RG 175 Blog)

Given that Rivers had to compete based on value, the focus on "how" was more tactical than strategic. Specifically, at Rivers, the "how" question inevitably led to obvious areas of the operation where it needed to invest. By far, the most important was the quality of the faculty. For Rivers to be successful, it had to focus on building an outstanding faculty. Thus, my attention initially was on retaining and recruiting a corps of teachers who could create experiences that would generate stories of excellence and at the same time, help to define "humanity" in ways that would fuel our differentiator. This top priority meant that I was involved significantly in all the hires. The stakes were simply too high. Without a significant proportion of "A -level" teachers, I fervently believed, Rivers would lose the game in the first inning. Thus, I paid close attention to hiring decisions.

I often read about the ill effects on senior administrators when a boss micromanages. And I've seen it. For leaders who can't help themselves, micromanaging builds mistrust and fails to leverage the talent of senior administrators. But a head, new to a school and knowing that the school needs significant changes, may be unsure about the hiring standards of veteran administrators. Under these circumstances, the adage "trust but verify" should inform the head's actions. For me, failing in this initial stage was not an option. In only a few cases did I usurp the lead in recruiting teachers in my first years at Rivers. More often, my close attention took the form of asking lots of questions, ensuring thorough vetting, asking how I could help in luring a top prospect, and talking to appropriate references. My focus showed senior leadership the high value I placed on talent. What a leader does over time eventually becomes valued; it seeps into the culture and becomes the norm.

Of course, bringing in new teachers and staff meant I had to let go of some people — never an easy job but essential if the head is going to signal that there is a new operational paradigm. In my first two years, I spent a lot of time with the school lawyer, discussing how to avoid lawsuits by not renewing contracts. This is not a job I relish, but if a head is going to "walk the talk" to signal that new standards are in place and that what worked in the past would no longer suffice, she must make the tough decisions early in her tenure. Rod Snelling argued that a new head has two years to make major personnel decisions. After that, the remaining teachers and staff are hers for the long haul, and she will have to live with the consequences of avoiding hard decisions early in her tenure. If quality teaching is a key element in your strategy, you must have difficult conversations sooner rather than later.

My early personnel moves raise the question of accountability in independent schools. In my experience, independent schools are quite responsive to parent and student complaints about teachers. As a result, those teachers in the "D" or "F" category are quickly moved out. My concern is the failure to address the problem of "B- "and "C+" teachers. The absence of clear standards and meaningful evaluation can mean that these teachers remain at the school for years. Accepting mediocrity and the unwritten rule, "Thou shalt not fire a teacher with more than five years of experience," can translate into "death by a thousand cuts" and a slow erosion of the value proposition.

What happens when a school takes inventory and realizes that a majority of its teachers are mediocre or slightly better? For some schools with teacher-proof students, this may not matter. They will get the results even though an opportunity to engage students and tap into their imaginations is lost.

Even mediocre teaching can't quench the thirst of ambitious and talented students.

But most schools don't fall into this category, and the cavalier approach to hiring and retaining excellence over the long haul can have a cumulative, devastating impact on the quality of education being offered. Ten years ago, Rob Evans wrote that thirty percent of the schools he worked with lacked a teacher evaluation program, and implementation was weak for many of the ones that did have a system. It amazes me that heads tout the special qualities of their teachers in talks to parents and prospective parents, extolling their dedication and at the same time, fail to create systems for meaningful professional growth and accountability.

On the other end of the spectrum, what do you think the benefits to a school would be if it had clear standards of teacher excellence, and seventy-five percent of the teachers fell into the "A" category? Would it be easier to raise money? Do you think the annual fund would go up? Would the head have more stories of excellence to share with trustees and prospective parents? And most importantly, would the power of positive word-of-mouth begin to weave its magic? A head needs to invest in story generators if she wants to improve the brand of the school and promote positive word-of-mouth. For most schools, those stories will be created by talented faculty members, who will use their creativity and skills to challenge and engage the students. Mediocrity is not a path to story generation. (Olverson, January 2016, RG 175 Blog)

For schools with established identities, complacency about recruiting and retaining talent is often the most obvious threat in the SWOT analysis. In these schools, increased faculty power and entitlement, combined with out-dated narratives extolling the virtues of the faculty, can lead to a slow decline. Confronting this reality is often difficult and thus, avoided. The long-term health of the school is sacrificed in order to avoid the short-term pain.

In addition to recruiting outstanding teachers, it would be imperative for Rivers to retain the 10 to 15 veteran teachers who embodied the essence of excellent teaching. There was no point in bringing in great faculty while watching outstanding teachers go out the door. I did not care about "my" teachers (the ones I hired) v. the "old guard." The school needed as much talent as it could get as quickly as possible. The retention of talent was, therefore, a top priority. We needed a new system to achieve this goal — more on this topic in the chapter on systems and structures.

You might be asking, "What about the administrators? Shouldn't attracting and retaining high-quality senior administrators be a central part of the "talent" strategy?" It's a logical question. However, I made the decision early in my tenure that with the limited money I had available, I needed to focus on retaining and attracting great teachers. Administrators were, like the teachers, woefully underpaid.

But limited resources require choices. I was laser-focused on building a great faculty that would produce the stories we needed in order to begin turning the ship. Focusing on the retention and recruitment of outstanding administrators was certainly tempting, but it would divert precious funds away from the investment in those that could generate stories - teachers. I took some flak for this decision, but strategy and its implementation are about making choices that align with the established goals and reflect a logical sequencing of actions given those goals. A thoughtfully constructed vision should easily translate into organizational priorities, leading to an appropriate allocation of resources. In independent schools with their village-like cultures, these decisions can lead to questions about fairness, especially when it comes to salaries. This questioning can produce moments of truth for a head. In choosing fairness over the proper allocation of limited resources to reach the strategic goals, the head might be making a decision to halt the change process and maintain the status quo. Choices are often about trade-offs and not without pain.

Another key component of the personnel strategy was hiring coaches who could turn around the athletic program. Again, limited funds handcuffed us; therefore, in consultation with the athletic director, we made some choices. We decided to allocate the limited money to recruiting top-tier coaches for two boys' and two girls' sports. We hoped that the coaches could recruit two-sport athletes who would, in turn, help some other teams. We needed coaches who were well-connected to strong student-athletes outside the school. For at least some of these coaches, our desire was to have them work full-time at the school, thus fostering positive relationships with the students and developing an understanding of the school's culture. In our ideal world, we wanted the coaches to recruit strong student-athletes who could trade up in the college admissions game and at the same time, begin helping the school develop a sense of pride through athletic success. We were open to the teacher-coach model for these four coaching positions if the teachers were good or excellent in the classroom, but we anticipated that we would have to create some staff positions for the new on-campus coaches to work full-time. The school would not deviate from the goal of a faculty consisting of mostly "A" teachers.

In truth, the pursuit of outstanding coaches had some potholes, but we never wavered from achieving the goal. The pursuit of big goals will inevitably involve some hiccups. Here's when the head and the relevant administrators require two attributes that today I constantly look for in head of school candidates: 1) the desire and ability to learn from mistakes and 2) a fierce determination to figure out the pathway to success. Setbacks are inevitable when a school is trying to accomplish big goals. The questions for leaders are: 1) will they learn from failures and adjust behavior, and 2) will they continue to hold themselves accountable for reaching the goals?

Another component of the athletic strategy was building a new athletic center. I knew that recruiting a handful of great coaches would not be enough to maximize our chances of attracting strong student-athletes. Rivers' athletic facility was small, dated, and significantly inferior to those of the other ISL schools. In addition, the school lacked a hockey rink and thus, could not offer girls' ice hockey, a burgeoning sport in New England at the time and one that we eventually targeted as one of our signature sports. Raising the money for an athletic center would be a monumental task but one well worth pursuing, given the stakes. It is important to note that real strategy almost always involves risk. In fact, if the leader doesn't feel as if she can lose, the strategy is probably too timid. Implementation often involves taking baby steps, but in the late 1990s, given the competition Rivers faced and the sense of urgency I tried to generate, I could not see how baby steps could help drive athletic excellence at the needed pace. We needed excellent coaches *and* athletic facilities for the school to be competitive in the ISL.

Another piece of the "how to" puzzle was finding a way to leverage a successful music school in order to attract skilled musicians and strong students. I knew the school's academic reputation needed to improve to attract the outstanding student musicians we wanted. But this fact did not obviate the immediate need for a plan. We could use the time to develop whatever program we were going to develop and refine it so that once we began attracting top student musicians, they would have a great experience. Here is where sequencing matters. The school's academic reputation would make it difficult to attract strong student musicians at the beginning. So, we needed to begin with strong musicians who were good or maybe just average students. As the academic profile of the school changed, we would be in a position to attract outstanding student musicians. The music school director and I spent hours generating possibilities for leveraging this asset.

Most of the conversations led to dead-ends. But deep conversations, although seemingly unproductive in the short run, often lead to creative long-term solutions. One day, the director came to my office and said, "I've got it." Thus, the Conservatory Program was born, a specialized after-school music program for talented musicians that advanced their skills and knowledge and gave them further opportunities to practice. In addition, the director decided to add a classical music component to the school's program that previously consisted primarily of instrumental jazz music. Wisely, he hired one of the top string teachers in the area and a member of the New England Conservatory's part-time faculty to start the program and recruit student musicians to the school.

In a previous chapter, I discussed the total overhaul of the Rivers Middle School. This overhaul resulted in a program that began our journey to define humanity at Rivers. As such, it turned out to be a vital vehicle for providing substance to "Excellence with Humanity." Because of the genius of our middle school head/architect, the program became a story generator beyond anything I could have imagined. In the early stages of the change efforts, these stories were often put on the back burner because of the difficult work of joining the constellation of strong schools and the fear that a "soft" middle school would compromise our excellence message. But once the school started gaining confidence, the stories from the middle school signaled to the market where Rivers was headed, and critical facets of its program began to make their way to the upper school. The journey was not without conflict between the upper and middle schools. As upper school teachers felt pressured to produce excellence, they saw the academic program in middle school as weak. But over time, this pressure dissipated. Upper school teachers who had students in the middle school began to understand its many benefits. Word spread throughout the faculty, and many teachers rightly began to see that the programs were complimentary in helping the school achieve its goals.

The specific strategies used at Rivers highlight the importance of results in designing a strategic plan. Specific, measurable results forced us to concentrate on two critical areas: teacher/coach quality and student talent. Only significant improvements in both areas would put the school in a position to achieve the desired results. A focus on results, though, requires the head to navigate conversations carefully and specifically, pay attention to the audience in communicating progress. Most trustees will embrace presentations with lots of statistics. These presentations touch a world that many of them are familiar with. Hence, presentations to the board were filled with data.

But educators are a different breed. In my experience, repeatedly presenting them with a lot of numbers in order to demonstrate the growing strength of the school can backfire. Occasional presentations to faculty about the school's successes can be useful, but when they devolve into a recitation of statistics, it can easily lead to cynicism and a narrative that the school is just another business. The head's EQ, particularly her deep understanding of what motivates excellent teachers, is vital in maintaining faculty morale. Excluding specialized schools in which skill development is so important, in my experience, high-performing teachers are motivated by the opportunity to create rich, intellectually challenging, and dynamic learning environments that prompt student inquiry and critical thinking. Having some number of students in the class who contribute to that environment is an absolute necessity. Presenting data to teachers about the growing selectivity of the school is just an abstraction. Instead, seeking out their stories about vibrant classrooms and energizing class discussions, the partial result of increased admissions selectivity, reminds them of why they entered this profession in the first place. The head must authentically share in the excitement of teachers. Successful heads know their audiences.

The beauty of *Playing to Win* is that it advocates for a leader who makes connections and creates coherent plans. As I read strategic plans on independent school websites, it's easy to get frustrated. First, many of them are similar to each other, a reflection of shallow thinking, often the result of mindlessly following a consultant's process designed to be quick, easy, and painless. The incoherence of these plans can be striking. One school established a goal of academic excellence without any indication of what was meant by the term. Its top strategy for attaining academic excellence was to hire a curriculum coordinator. Under academic excellence, the school also listed the strengthening of social-emotional learning. Now, I have no problem per se with curriculum coordinators and social-emotional learning, but where is the connection to academic excellence? By not defining academic excellence, leadership could include trendy initiatives that had something to do with teaching and learning. Everybody gets to include their favorite educational fads, and all are happy. This is not an example of strategic thinking; it's simply a wish list of random items, and as such, has no power to significantly improve the school and establish a clear and compelling brand.

Finally, it's worth repeating that the head's ability to tap into the imaginations of those with whom she works can produce results far beyond what the head imagined. Looking back, I am struck by how obvious the establishment of the Conservatory Program seems. But the hours of conversation in search of some way to leverage the music school was necessary in order for the music school director to formulate the idea. I don't believe in lightning bolts of imagination; more often than not, hard work, conversation, and lots of thinking take us to the edge where imagination kicks in. In addition, the music school's decision to hire the string teacher from New England Conservatory to develop the chamber music program was a page right out of the handbook for building a strong athletic program- hire talented coaches who can attract student athletes who will create stories of excellence. Steve Jobs' quote about how creativity works captures an essential pathway to creating value:

Creativity is just connecting things. When you ask creative people how they did something, they feel a little guilty because they didn't really do it, they just saw something. It seemed obvious to them after a while. That's because they were able to connect experiences they've had and synthesize new things.

Observing, conversing, grappling, connecting, and learning — all create a culture that promotes creative thinking, which, in turn, provides the blueprint for achieving ambitious goals.

Questions

1. What pricing strategy must the school develop, given the vision and market?

2. How will you develop the plan? Who will be involved and why?

3. What are the critical elements of the plan? Will success in these areas lead to the realization of the vision and a strengthening of the school's brand?

4. How will you roll out the plan and will the roll-out create significant pushback?

5. Are the appropriate assets of the school being leveraged to support the strategy?

Reader's Notes

Chapter 7

Execution: Where Strategic Plans Go to Die

The genius of *Playing to Win* lies in its comprehensive approach to strategy, its emphasis on both the dreams and the practical realities. There are so many reasons strategic plans fall short, but one of the most frequent is the failure of leadership to account for the school's ability to execute, both in terms of its capabilities and systems. This key component of strategy is precisely why Martin and Lafley insist that no answer to one of the five questions be finalized until that answer's impact on the other questions is considered.

In the independent school world, assessing capabilities and systems and their possible relevance to achieving goals is an essential component in the SWOT analysis. Capabilities and systems can fall under strengths or weaknesses. In achieving the school's strategic goals, some capabilities and structures are relevant, even vital, and some are not. In this regard, one of Martin and Lafley's central questions becomes a powerful tool: *If the organization is to achieve a specific goal, what needs to be true?* This question forces leadership to design backward and should ultimately lead to identifying those organizational elements critical to executing a plan.

Once capabilities and systems have been identified, leadership can assess their relevance. The SWOT analysis reveals the existing toolbox for the head. As she formulates strategies, she knows what's in the toolbox, and therefore, what can be achieved, and cannot be achieved, given the tools she has. In addition, she can determine which capabilities need investment so they can be leveraged to achieve the vision.

By way of example, to increase faculty salaries and jump-start change, Rivers needed money. Despite some limited accumulated reserves, we decided to maximize the potential of the annual fund as quickly as possible in order to achieve the school's ambitious goals. Without increased monies from a growing annual fund, the school would not have the fuel to drive and sustain change. In 1997, I was under no illusion that the annual fund could provide an unlimited source of revenue. Fundraising, to a large extent, is determined by the strength of the school's brand. Thus, Rivers' reputation placed a ceiling on how much it could raise in the near future. And yet, given the need for additional money in order to raise salaries, the school had to reach that ceiling — the upper limit of what could be raised annually. I wasn't sure what that ceiling was, but the director of development and I believed it was higher than the current giving indicated.

But investing time and energy to strengthen a needed capability may not produce the desired results immediately. In fact, if the head is playing the long game and focused on sustainability, then the fruits of investment will probably take some time to materialize. Thankfully, the fiscal stewardship of the business manager at Rivers and the $2 million accumulated surplus resulting from that stewardship provided a critical bridge to a more robust annual fund. The business manager's frugality allowed the school to jump-start faculty salary increases, but it would be a few years later before the annual fund could sustain these increases. Herein lies a perfect illustration of the importance of the SWOT. It identifies valuable tools that can be leveraged to execute the plan.

With the strategic imperative in mind, the development director and I decided we needed to focus on big gifts instead of participation. This tactic made sense not only for the purpose of raising more money but also in light of the fact that the school's new direction somewhat disaffected significant numbers of parents. In addition, we needed more robust giving from trustees. This meant asking existing trustees for more money and recruiting new ones with philanthropic capacity.

Furthermore, the school had not leveraged a key skill that the board chair possessed – asking major donors for large gifts. He enjoyed asking for money and brought credibility to the table because of his substantial giving. Making the ask is one of the most important skills needed on a board and is often overlooked by new heads.

Turning our attention to systems, the development director and I began to change the composition of the board's development committee. More importantly, we convinced the board to create a sub-committee called major gifts. Because this was a new committee, we had more influence over determining its composition and could move faster in developing and executing plans. The result was a committee with members that had extensive giving capacity and often knowledge of those in the Rivers community who had similar capacity. This knowledge was invaluable as we learned about a potential donor's interests, what she thought of the school, and any recent developments in her business that might impact giving. This information and a renewed focus on donor research helped paint a more complete picture of our major donors.

The major gifts committee personalized annual fund solicitations with significant donors. Its members helped strategize approaches — who was the best person to do the ask, what number should we be looking at, and what role should I play? The development director, who understood major gifts and the importance of cultivation, relationship-building, and research, was instrumental in strengthening our fundraising capacity. A successful fundraiser at Boston University, she understood that at the same time she was directing the members of the major gifts sub-committee to focus on other donors, she was cultivating them and increasing their emotional investment in achieving fundraising goals and advancing the school.

When talent and the correct structure come together, success is usually the result. The creation of the major gifts committee, combined with the expertise of the development director, meant that the right people were focused on work that would make a significant difference to the school. Most importantly, the structure clearly had a purpose that connected to the overall strategy to jump-start change — building a strong faculty. This work did not happen overnight; it took four to five years to refine our tactics and see the fruits of the investment.

For Rivers, focusing on the annual fund as a mechanism for fueling change made sense. But schools with different circumstances may focus on other potential capabilities. Summer camp revenue, tuition increases, cost-cutting measures, and short-term limited borrowing are a handful of ways to generate income to invest in the realization of a strategic goal. Furthermore, investments may not require additional funds. Every school's circumstances are different in magnitude and scope and thus, require different tactics. The key is to identify the school's assets as a way to envision how they might be used to create value.

Establishing systems and structures signals that a school desires sustainable change by continually improving practices to achieve goals. Implicit in the creation of structures is institutional learning, a critical element if a school is to realize its vision. But structures are not a panacea; they are not a substitute for talent, and they can often devolve into bureaucracy. However, well designed structures have the power to promote communication, connect action to purpose, and tap the collective genius of the team. They are a crucial management tool for long-term school improvement but only if their work is connected to achieving the vision.

In "The One Type of Leader Who Can Turn Around a Failing School" (Harvard Business Review, October 2016), Alex Hill, Liz Mellon, Ben Laker, and Jules Goddard studied 411 British educational leaders. The four researchers conducted interviews, delved into their subjects' experiences and backgrounds, and assessed each leader's long-term performance based on specific measurements valued in British education. The authors discovered five leader types, but the one kind of leader who had the longest-lasting impact was the architect. Architect-leaders take the long view, and this is absolutely critical for sustainable change. They don't think in terms of immediate solutions, often designed to make leaders look good; they believe in systems that promote long-term collaboration, imagination, and problem-solving. They don't see themselves as the "answer man." They build infrastructure that supports talented people talking with each other about issues that matter. In short, they are building the foundation for excellence based on vision, talent, and structure. The value they bring to a school is positive, sustainable change that lasts because the systems put in place promote ongoing improvement and continued focus on the realization of the vision. (Olverson, May 2017, RG 175 Blog)

Structures often entail getting the right people in the same room to talk about meaningful subjects, with the vision acting as a driving backdrop. Achieving results is often easier when these meetings are within a department or between department leaders and the head. They can become much more difficult when they involve two or more departments. In my discovery visits to schools as part of the head search process, I often hear staff and faculty using the word "siloed" to describe the absence of internal communications.

Using the lens of an architect-leader (facilitating execution through structures) allows the head to design structures in ways that mitigate the tendency toward organizational silos. At Rivers, we put most of our eggs in the high-performing-faculty basket supported by a stronger annual fund. Most of the work designed to enhance the annual fund fell within the development office. But there was a critical opportunity that the school could not overlook in this effort - admissions.

The school needed admissions and development working together to identify and assess potential major donors whose children were applying. The development office used its network to identify these families, and often, the admissions office gained a sense of which families might be helpful in fundraising. Information flow between the two departments was crucial. The school was not going to compromise admission standards for children of wealthy families, but early assessments of students from these families could help mobilize cultivation strategies and create touch points that might ultimately lead to enrollment.

Before the focus on the annual fund, there was very little communication between admissions and development. But as fundraising became a priority, both departments needed to work together. And they did so successfully. The key to success was the clarity of the vision and strategy. Both directors understood that the school needed stronger students and teachers (meaning higher salaries). There was no possible misunderstanding about the purpose of working together.

In so many dysfunctional schools, the head fails to articulate purpose, allowing senior administrators to drift into protecting their turf. This failure is one of frequency as well. A head cannot just articulate once why it is important for two departments to work together; she needs to articulate it repeatedly. The psychology of leading requires the head to understand the natural proclivities of human beings, and their desire to protect power is one of them. To this end, in schools that are trying to capture a market position, the head should not be delegating this task to an assistant head for external relations who oversees departments like development and admissions. That level of bureaucracy lends itself to the use of power and authority instead of passion and persuasion to promote collaboration. Any value in coordinating the efforts of these two departments is offset by the absence of vision and purpose. The school might get lucky and hire a true leader for that position, but in my experience, it engages someone who thinks her job is to have authority over other departments. As is often the case, the structure is put in place because it existed at the head's former school or is popular at the "best" schools. This reasoning increases authority but kills motivation, especially for schools that are trying to capture or strengthen a market niche.

Rivers' focus on the annual fund as necessary in executing a sustainable faculty salary plan highlights the importance of prioritizing goals. The school had to invest in capabilities critical for achieving this goal. The establishment of the major gifts committee provided a new structure that fostered conversations that led to actions that made a difference. Effective systems breed results. They put the right people in the right conversations, creating value for the school.

New heads should remember that not all operations need their attention early on. I paid very little attention to the work of the various parent volunteer organizations at the school, not because I was unappreciative but because I needed to concentrate on those capabilities vital to reaching the winner's circle. There is often pressure for heads to spread their attention around, and of course, completely ignoring elements of the operation is unwise. However, where the head focuses her attention is a choice, one that must be intentional and aligned with the strategy.

The benefits of focusing initially on the annual fund went beyond the additional money raised. It created the foundation for a successful capital campaign in the early 2000s, that led to the construction of the athletic center. That building was vital to achieving one of the school's strategic goals. Bigger annual fund gifts led donors to set their sights higher and invest in the school's success. It also revealed new major donors. Rivers needed tangible and immediate results from the annual fund for faculty salaries, but it also needed a mechanism to identify major donors in order to achieve even bigger fundraising goals. The annual fund enhanced the school's capability to achieve in the short term while establishing a foundation for the long term. Successful execution can lead to new opportunities. Again, deep thinking about the question, "What needs to be true in order to achieve this goal?" lends itself to thinking about the sequencing of initiatives in order to achieve desired results. In the case of Rivers, a strong annual fund was a necessary prerequisite for a successful capital campaign — the case for most independent schools.

There are some key takeaways from this effort to enhance the annual fund. First, the vision, blessed by the board, enables the leader to look down the road, see what is needed to achieve the goals, and then make the necessary investments to enhance capabilities in the areas that matter most. Second, leading is about making choices. In developing the board, we could have used any number of criteria to determine, with the committee on trustees, the composition of the board — loyalty to the school, willingness to volunteer, diversity, and alumni engagement. All of these could be legitimate factors in selecting new trustees. But none, in Rivers' particular case, would lead the school to the winner's circle, as defined by the vision. I took some criticism for pushing the committee on trustees to focus on the prospective trustee's wealth, but criticism is inevitable and will come with trying to achieve something significant. The point is that vision can't be just a collection of inspiring words; its power lies in informing day-to-day decision-making.

By the time I began pushing harder for my agenda, I had earned some credibility that enhanced confidence in my leadership and gave me more clout at trustee meetings.

However, I never assumed that I could move forward without the support of the board. Thus, the director of development and I established game plans to make the case for our desired trustee choices. Often, this involved one-on-one meetings with key trustees. In particular, I did not want to assume that my growing power should be a substitute for the hard work of developing consensus within the board. Nor did I want to distance myself from the board and assume that strengthening it was not my responsibility.

I have seen too many heads adopt this latter approach. They work with senior administrators and the board to establish plans but fail to see that without a strong board, implementation is compromised. Then these same heads blame the trustees when the goals are not achieved: "Well, the board just doesn't get it."

In many cases, the strategic plan ends up on a shelf. If the head wants the school to win, she must own every step of the journey that leads to victory, including shaping the board of trustees as a critical asset to realizing the vision. Different heads will have different approaches to what that ownership looks like, including persuading trustees to take the lead in advocating necessary actions. I am not proposing that the head abandon the strategic partnership with the board; the head has to build consensus and have the board vet proposed initiatives. But simply ignoring the composition of the board as a critical component in successful implementation is short-sighted. I have witnessed too many heads who would rather be right by staying in their lanes according to "best practices," than win.

In assessing capabilities during the SWOT analysis, it's easy for first-time heads to ignore the importance of the board. Trustees, collectively and individually, have the capacity to generate and accelerate positive change, adding enormous value to a school. Of course, the most obvious way this happens is through philanthropy, but tapping into their talents, expertise, and skills can produce significant benefits to the school.

I witnessed a perfect illustration of a trustee bringing value to the table. As Rivers sought town approvals for building a 72,000-square-foot athletic center, it naturally aroused the concern of some neighbors. Led by a land-use lawyer who was not working at the time, the neighbors became more and more contentious, especially as they imagined the late-night rentals of a hockey rink to beer-drinking adults. One of our trustees, a highly successful developer who understood our town's politics, joined me at a planning board meeting as the school sought a curb cut for the athletic center project. Without this approval, we could not build the athletic center. For an hour, I was pilloried by neighbors. I was seething; why didn't the trustee defend me? During a break, he quietly went up to the planning board members and asked for the curb-cut approval. They voted for approval, and as we walked to our cars, he said with a smile on his face, "We got the approval." He later explained that neighbor attacks are often the norm and the organization's leader should not respond, which only serves to escalate the tension. His deft handling of the situation, rooted in his deep experience and expertise, helped the school achieve a critical victory. (Olverson, November 2016, RG 175 Blog)

Strengthening the school's board of trustees as part of enhancing a critical capability raises questions about the criteria for trusteeship and the purpose trustees should serve? Countless articles have been written about boards behaving badly or rogue trustees not being held accountable. In the last three years, there has been more talk about unplanned head departures, which is code for heads being fired. I have heard the stories about boards out of control, and I have certainly heard about trustees stepping over that proverbial line between administration and governance. But sometimes, unwitting culprits in these ugly stories are the heads of school themselves because they don't help the committee on trustees connect the dots between future success and the strength of the board.

In working with the committee on trustees to identify future trustees, heads need to insist that the committee articulate the value the prospective trustee will bring to the table. That value should normally be more than just wealth, as important as that can be. Identifying value is made so much easier when the head generates a clear vision and strategy in partnership with the board or when a critical capability needs to be strengthened. In short, potential trustees must help the school get to the winner's circle and bring their skills, expertise, wealth, and/or clout to support the school in achieving its vision. They should not simply be a bunch of bosses exercising authority over the head. (Olverson, February 2020, RG 175 Blog)

In addition, they need to know why they are being asked to join the board, their general responsibilities in ensuring that the mission is being fulfilled, and, most importantly, the nature of their workflow. They need to know when the workload will be light and when it will be heavy, depending on the task at hand and the need for their skills and expertise. If heads don't want new trustees to play school, trustees need to understand the nature of their jobs, specifically under what circumstances their expertise becomes vital and under what circumstances it lies dormant.

Despite the many positives a potential trustee may bring to the board, the head and the committee on trustees must also examine the downsides. For a current parent, it may be a child who struggles academically, leading to requests for exemptions or special favors in return for support. Perhaps a wealthy alum wants to resurrect a dead program, clarifying that her giving is predicated on the school taking action. In short, "keeping your eyes on the prize" may inadvertently distract the committee and the head from serious downsides that will cause major headaches down the road. "Seeing around the corner" is a vital skill for heads of school.

By increasing the school's capability to generate revenue through the annual fund, Rivers could now turn to strengthening faculty performance as the critical component in achieving "Excellence with Humanity." The initial goal was simple: retain and recruit outstanding teachers through increased salaries and inform underperformers that their contracts would not be renewed. Although these actions were a critical first step in implementing strategy, they lacked the capability of *sustaining* excellent performance, which was vital to capturing the desired market niche.

In order to play the long game and sustain high performance, we needed a system. We were not convinced that raising salaries guaranteed long-term, enhanced performance. We didn't want to raise teachers' salaries just to be nice, although we felt that teachers were incredibly undervalued in our country. Yes, salaries would increase the chances of attracting and retaining top talent. But we had seen schools that created lofty faculty salary goals in their strategic plans, implemented those goals, but never determined if those increased salaries actually raised performance. Rivers didn't want a proxy for high performance; it wanted high performance.

To feel confident that higher salaries would make a long-term difference in clarifying the school's identity, we wanted to 1) define excellent teaching at Rivers and 2) incentivize faculty to perform at the highest levels based on Rivers' definition of excellent teaching. The school didn't have time to slowly create a faculty culture of excellence.

Thus, I formed a committee of two outstanding teachers and myself, and we created a career ladder. First, we tackled the criteria for evaluating performance. We came up with eleven standards, including some critical ones: a) evidence of challenging students with high standards, b) evidence of engaging students, c) evidence of communicating through words and actions that the teacher wants the student to be successful, and d) evidence that the teacher cares about students. These were among the behaviors that would be critical in fulfilling our brand promise. Our committee was not interested in dictating teaching methods or robbing teachers of the autonomy that independent schools value. The focus was on results, which aligned with our emerging definition of "Excellence with Humanity."

With the career ladder, teachers could, at designated times in their careers and at their discretion, undergo an assessment that would lead to a significant increase in salary in addition to the standard annual increase. The most frequently sought-after professional step on the ladder was senior teacher. If, after a two-person evaluation of a teacher, she was elevated to "senior teacher" status, she received an eight percent permanent salary increase on top of the standard annual raise. We outlined a process for application and limited the number of evaluations to three to four per year based on the budget and the time needed to complete the thorough evaluations.

We encouraged an outstanding veteran teacher to be the first applicant, and she became our first senior teacher. The second applicant went through the process, and we turned him down. He left a year later. The rejection of his application lent credibility to the system's integrity, signaling to the teachers that we were intent on adhering to the eleven standards. Over the years, we tweaked the system, but the principles remained the same: 1) a clear definition of excellent teaching that reflected the strategic direction of the school and 2) a commitment to rewarding it. One of the tweaks included an endorsement of the application from the division head, which had the added benefit of encouraging honest conversations about performance and growth areas.

Moreover, senior teachers fulfilled additional responsibilities by mentoring new teachers. Included in this work were classroom visits and feedback sessions, the content of which was strictly confidential between the senior teacher and the mentee. In this way, the school was able to energize outstanding veteran teachers as they began to own some responsibility for their role in building an excellent faculty that would get the school to the winner's circle. Success leads to new opportunities; the virtuous cycle is unleashed.

Systems influence behaviors. When systems are thoughtfully constructed to change behavior, they can overcome stasis. The key is being intentional and knowing the "why" of your system. Effective systems connect daily behavior to vision. This is their real value.

In contrast, one-off actions lack the power to sustain desired behavior. I know of one head who understood that his teachers needed to raise their standards for students. His response was to write notes on the bottom of their contracts, encouraging them to raise the bar. It had no impact on teacher behavior. Why should it have? It failed to account for the magnitude of the challenge and how years of practice calcified attitudes.

New heads need to analyze school culture and its supporting systems that impact behavior so they can assess the school's capacity to execute. Changes in those systems or the addition of new systems should derive from the school's strategy. To ignore this aspect of the change effort is a prescription for unrealized dreams, which, in turn, often morphs into faculty cynicism.

Effective creation of systems is ultimately about alignment between day-to-day behavior in the trenches and the vision and strategic goals that guide the school. In this regard, alignment represents a powerful lens through which a head can examine behavior to determine if that behavior is helping the school achieve its goals. A leader knows that alignment exists if daily behavior produces stories that can be used to reinforce the brand and sell the school.

Of course, the pursuit of one goal should not preclude pursuing opportunities as they arise. Early in my tenure at Rivers, despite focusing on excellence, I was open to tangible ways to demonstrate humanity. I realized the school had adopted a relatively standard upper-school course selection practice. Students sat down with advisors in the spring and chose courses for the following year. But with the introduction of more honors and AP courses and electives, I saw an opportunity to demonstrate a more personalized approach that would show our parents the degree to which we knew their children.

The idea came from watching our director of college counseling, who, in the initial meeting with parents and their children, worked with the students to select courses for the senior year. This feature of the meeting was not simply an add-on; it was intimately tied to the student's college interests, athletic/arts schedule, the student's passions, and more. The director of college counseling could have this conversation with the student in front of the parents because he had done his homework. I sat in on meetings and saw the counselor engender trust and strengthen his credibility with students and parents. Channeling Steve Jobs on creativity (copy ideas from other domains), I thought, why not use a variation of this system for all upper school students to customize their respective schedules and demonstrate our deep knowledge of them in front of parents?

Thus, the course counseling system was born with designated course counselors for each upper school grade level. The approach to course counseling varied by grade, but the intent was always the same: customize the student's course selection and create a "high touch" opportunity that reflected humanity.

The point is not for schools to adopt Rivers' course counseling system. It is, rather, for the leadership of a school to examine tired systems in order to find opportunities to advance the desired goals.

As was the case with the annual fund, leveraging opportunities can often lead to new opportunities. A major added benefit to course counseling was the chance to hear a student comment on her overall experience during the current year. Although a parent was typically present, the conversation was between the student and counselor. The meetings created an effective feedback system, far more nuanced than surveys, as the counselor would often begin with "Tell me how the year has been for you. What's been good, and what has not gone so well?" The program was time-intensive, but in my mind, "Excellence with Humanity" had to be substantive; we wanted more than a tagline. We wanted actual experiences.

Over the years, the school devised other systems with the specific intent of personalizing the student experience. I had little involvement in the creation of these systems. Administrators and faculty generated the ideas and implemented them. In a perfect example of how systems and practices influence faculty culture, the middle school head, in the weekly faculty meetings, asked teachers to talk about students they were concerned about and students who had stood out positively. It was such a simple structure, one that many schools use. But its power was immense. In these meetings, teachers learned how to talk constructively about students, be positive in describing their growth, and brainstorm strategies to help struggling students. In talking about the students, they were, in effect, reminding themselves why they got in this business in the first place — to make a positive difference in the lives of children. "Excellence with Humanity" in action! The middle school head created the structure and the rules, and faculty behavior and culture changed.

One of the benefits of a clear vision is that it provides decision-makers with a context that helps them to make decisions with the end game in mind. At Rivers, we invested in the annual fund to provide a stream of money to support the recruitment and retention of talent. This was the cornerstone of our strategy. We embraced policies and practices that supported that goal. In my first year at Rivers, as I was working on the annual fund and faculty salary plan, the board's personnel committee continued its work from the previous year with the intent of eliminating tuition remission. The committee had studied other schools' policies and viewed the issue through a financial lens and through a fairness lens. Without a vision, there was certainly an argument for its elimination. What about teachers without children? What about teachers who would not qualify for financial aid?

I understood. But for the goals we wanted to achieve, the possible unfairness of the policy took a back seat to retaining and attracting great teachers right away. Increasing salaries and then eliminating a major benefit seemed like two steps forward and one step backward. We needed all three steps to go forward. I convinced the committee to continue the tuition remission policy for up to two children, thus preserving an important tool in the quest to attract and retain the best. Once again, the mere existence of a tangible goal informed decision-making. In a different context, the school's decision may not have been right. But given what the school was trying to achieve, preserving tuition remission made complete sense.

I suspect that for many heads of school, an assessment of the school's capabilities and systems never happens. Many have simply not been taught to think deeply about execution and its connection to vision and strategic goals. For first-time heads, here are some key questions that may lead to valuable insights about the school's capacity to execute:

- How strong is the board, and in what areas?

- Is the business office capable of creating increasingly refined financial models that provide a credible means for stress-testing future strategic moves?

- As giving capacity increases, can the development office organize efforts to take advantage of this newly created capacity, including developing strategies for major gifts?

- Can the enrollment management office use research to refine strategies for capturing targeted families and strengthening the school's brand?

- Can the enrollment management office use research to gain deeper insights into attrition and develop strategies for addressing it, including, if appropriate, a thoughtful examination of the value proposition?

- Can most teachers create the desired student experiences and outcomes that reinforces the desired brand?

- Do all managers have a clear understanding of what excellent performance looks like and do they use that understanding to create a culture of accountability?

- Which departments need to be talking with each other, and how can the head motivate these departments to move beyond parochial concerns?

Given the school's specific circumstances, the head may need to focus on capabilities other than the ones above, but the list provides an entry point. Critical to assessing capabilities is the relative value of each capability to jumpstart change.

With limited resources, schools have to make choices. In my first few years at Rivers, it would have been great to have an experienced, high-functioning marketing department. But based on what the school was trying to achieve, there were other more compelling capabilities the school needed to invest in. Herein lies an easy trap for new heads to fall into — spreading resources (time, energy, and money) around so that everyone is happy. Once a head does this, she has diminished the capacity to achieve the most important goals. Heads have to prioritize.

It may be tempting for new heads to ignore the school's capabilities and structures as they determine the strengths and weaknesses of the school, but they do so at their own peril. Heading a school is like conducting an orchestra. When the conductor is ready to feature a section of the orchestra, she has to know that it will perform at a high level. The conductor can hide and feature based on the capabilities of each section. But if a particular section of the orchestra is absolutely necessary, and it is not capable of performing at a high level, the conductor has to invest in that section to ensure quality execution. Otherwise, she must change the piece that the orchestra is playing.

There is nothing earth-shattering about the structures we used at Rivers. Many independent schools have similar committees and practices. But focusing on the existence of a structure captures only part of its significance. What matters is its connection to strategy, the role it plays in achieving the "winning aspiration." Structures informed by purpose and vision are necessary for success because they make behavior intentional. The "why" is front and center, and actions naturally flow from it. Conversely, new heads that establish structures without a clear strategic intent may unwittingly be creating a path to inertia and cynicism.

Looking at the school through the lens of capability allows a new head to determine where investments of time, energy, and money will be required to execute the strategy successfully. In addition, examining structures can lead to the discovery of insidious inhibitors of change, such as tired practices, useless meetings, policies that stifle imagination, outdated narratives, and more. In the final analysis, it's easy to dream; it's harder to execute. British army officer Colonel T.E. Lawrence once wrote:

> "All men dream, but not equally. Those who dream by night in the dusty recesses of their minds, wake in the day to find that it was vanity; but the dreamers of the day are dangerous men, for they may act on their dreams with open eyes, to make them possible."

Questions

1. What capabilities are necessary for realizing the vision? Personnel, fund raising, financial models, program, board of trustees, communications, facilities? Which ones need investment and why?

2. What existing structures are inhibiting change? Where are the silos? How will you break them down?

3. To what extent will the board be an asset in achieving the strategic goals? Does the composition of the board need attention?

4. Is the quality and nature of the daily work of faculty and staff connected to the realization of the vision? Are stories that capture the essence of the school being generated? Are they being told?

5. Can you articulate the "why" of your structures? Does their work support the vision?"

<u>Reader's Notes</u>

Chapter 8

Leadership Is More Than Strategy

Looking at leadership through the lens of strategy provides a powerful tool for heads to help their schools better live their missions and achieve sustainable change. Although I am an enthusiastic proponent of *Playing to Win,* a rigid, lock-step implementation of the five guiding principles ignores other key elements in leading an independent school, elements that are critical in successfully devising and implementing strategy. Some of these elements of leadership are intuitive; some can be learned by mistakes and subsequent learning, and others can be observed in admired leaders. These leadership elements are the mortar that holds strategic thinking together.

Discipline- Intentionally and consistently exercising discipline in formulating and executing strategy is critical to success. Real strategy emerges from a deep understanding of the school. In talking to a group of parents at a school where there had been five heads in ten years, there was strong sentiment that the next head, unlike some of the previous ones, not come in with a specific agenda before understanding the school. This is why the SWOT is so important; it provides the head a deep knowledge of the school that she must have as a foundation for thinking strategically. At this particular school, the most recent head became excited about social-emotional learning and allied with some teachers who were also enthusiastic about this approach to education. This is a classic case of a head inflicting her values on the school without asking, "What does the school need?" The leader's passion should align with the needs of the school. It should never dictate.

How would you feel about a doctor who prescribed a treatment for you without even exploring your condition? Her reasoning is that she's really excited about the treatment plan. Schools are not vessels in which heads can express their deeply-held beliefs about education without acknowledging that the schools have their histories, unique challenges, unique cultures, and aspirations. These challenges and aspirations need to factor into strategic thinking. Most importantly, the new head must take the time and exercise the discipline to understand the school at a deep level. It's this understanding that serves as a wellspring for imagination and vision. Creating value involves starting slowly and eventually moving faster, emphasizing understanding before taking action.

Discipline also means executing the strategy when it is tempting to pivot. There is a critical moment in a successful organization's evolution. Having achieved table stakes status or at least demonstrating that it is clearly on the path to earning this status, the organization is now left with the question, "What's next?" I cannot over-emphasize the importance of this moment for independent schools.

At Rivers, we secured talent, established programs, strengthened capabilities, and created structures — all for the purpose of joining the constellation of good and great schools that constituted the ISL. Rivers had yet to fully attain "table stakes" status regarding academic, athletic, and artistic excellence, but it was clearly moving in that direction with results to prove it. Now, the moment of truth. Did the school have the discipline to maintain the "table-stakes" path while intentionally building its differentiator, humanity? Success has a way of debilitating discipline. The lessons learned from success can intoxicate leadership as a school gets closer to the glitter associated with the most elite schools. I was determined not to let that happen at Rivers.

Nine years into my tenure, we thought it was time to focus on "Humanity" by working on a new strategic plan that would generate programs that illustrated the school's commitment to the whole child. Initially, we fell into the trap of following the traditional independent school playbook. The school hired a consultant, held a retreat, and identified what leadership thought the school should tackle next. It was a colossal waste of time. After several months of discussion, the board instructed me to establish and present the goals for board approval. After soliciting opinions from the faculty and staff, I did so, and Rivers began to work on establishing its differentiator.

My direct involvement in implementing this strategy was limited, except in fundraising for a campus center. Faculty and administrators jumped at the chance to build programs that would distinguish Rivers. The upper school head tackled the schedule and spent two years working with a faculty committee to design a modified block schedule. The result was less student and faculty stress, more engaged students, and happier parents. The school counselor and the middle school head became excited about student leadership after attending professional development workshops. Both promoted interest in leadership as a mechanism for creating a positive school culture and graduating students who embraced the qualities of high moral and performance character. An English teacher became excited about interdisciplinary studies as a vehicle for real-world learning. He developed a relationship with the guru of interdisciplinary studies at the Harvard Graduate School of Education, who guided the school's efforts in building this new department. From it came a dynamic program in partnership with the Harvard Center for Bioethics, which led to students grappling with the complex moral dilemmas that medical clinicians often face. The assistant head worked with an upper school committee of teachers to revamp the upper school advisor program and establish a dean system at each grade level to ensure that structures existed that could easily shine a light on any student in the upper school. His committee also created the parent-advisor conference that allowed the school to demonstrate how well it knew the students in addition to establishing a partnership with parents.

As this burst of creativity emerged, my job was simple: 1) maintain the focus on excellence so that this key dimension of the school's emerging identity and table stakes strategy was not compromised and 2) encourage the faculty and administrators by finding professional development money, taking an active interest in what they were creating, and giving them air time at faculty meetings to sell their ideas and get others excited.

I did get involved in the planning and fundraising for a new campus center in order to promote humanity. The school's concept of humanity included a strong sense of community, and as was the case with athletics, facilities played a critical role. As the Rivers' enrollment grew, it was obvious that the absence of adequate all-school, division, and small group gathering spaces was limiting community connections.

The school often used the gym, where the acoustics were horrible. All-school and division assemblies were critical in creating a culture of inclusivity, a sense of pride as students began to earn athletic and arts awards, and an opportunity to connect the two divisions through shared experiences. After the construction of the campus center, the school community enjoyed some memorable student instrumental performances as the Conservatory Program began to generate excellence. The performances created a sense of inclusion, helping the Conservatory students feel a stronger connection to the larger school community.

As is the case with any brand-building, a comprehensive approach is critical to success. The advisor program, assemblies, a dining room, student leadership, diversity programs, and a new schedule demonstrated that Rivers was a school that believed in humanity. But most importantly, the school exercised the discipline to stay the course and create a true differentiator rather than mindlessly trying to imitate the elite schools. The head must believe in her game plan no matter the temptation to deviate.

Discipline also entails consensus-building as the foundation for sustainable change. Entrepreneurial heads must resist the temptation to move forward without consensus, especially with their boards. Consensus does not mean that all are in favor of the direction the head is proposing to take the school, but the naysayers have to be neutralized by a vast and enthusiastic majority who want to jump on the head's bandwagon. Until that magic number is reached, the head has to continue to win support for the vision. The process of building consensus is also the foundation for successfully implementing the plan. Trustees and other key stakeholders see the head's vision and want to play a role in realizing it. Taking the time to build consensus is an opportunity to sell the plan and generate enthusiasm for its implementation.

Trustees should not be the only target of consensus-building. Schools are strange organizations. Faculty can wield power as well. Some might argue that the widely revered fourth-grade teacher, who taught trustee and alumni children, has more power than a first-year head. There is little question that a first-year head has to intentionally earn respect and credibility as a leader before exercising power. In order to rally faculty and staff support for the new vision, new heads should consider the following:

1. Identify the primary influencers and power brokers among the faculty and staff and use them as weather gauges to test key elements of the vision. Make the influencers show their cards early, and take the time to win them over. Don't be subservient in your approach or transactional; you are still the head of school. If there is resistance among the influencers, you may need to strategize with others, but don't ever think that by virtue of your sitting in the head's chair, you can wave a wand to make real change happen within the faculty.

2. Through conversations, challenge the teachers to use their experience and imagination to help realize the vision. Often, teachers become bored and cynical because they are not challenged or asked to help the school reach its destination. That's on the head. I once listened to a first-time head talk about his veteran teachers resisting a workshop on design

thinking. As I listened, I thought to myself, "Why is this head forcing the faculty to endure workshops on design thinking? This kind of workshop should be coming from the faculty." It was painful listening to this head. He went to a conference, became excited about design thinking, and decided that his school, in an effort to keep up, needed to do this work as well. But there was no reason except to keep up with the competition, an explanation that will typically not motivate educators. Leadership is not about the leader; it's about the followers and followers need a plausible "why."

3. Tap into the original reasons for educators to get into this business — to make a difference in children's lives. Many of them teach in independent schools because they don't want the rigidity of the public school system. But over time, it's easy to fall into ruts and take the path of least resistance. Heads can counter this tendency by presenting a vision, purposely leaving much of the canvas blank, asking the educators to fill it in, and incentivizing this work.

Of course, to accomplish this goal, you need to be an effective communicator. Some heads are gifted orators who can win over a crowd with charm, wit, and stories. This skill is a powerful tool for building consensus and sharing passion. Others are more effective in one-on-one situations, in which they tailor the case to the person they are talking to. Whether your strength is one-on-one or public speaking or both, you must convince key stakeholders that they will play a vital role in achieving greatness. This is leadership.

Urgency- Given my admonitions about discipline and patience, you may understandably be confused. Taking the time to establish a consensus about the vision and the broad plan of action to achieve the vision is the critical foundation for success. However, once this consensus has been established, the head must drive change by putting it front and center so that the key players involved in implementation keep their focus on achieving the goals. Although the head may be removed by one or two layers from implementation at larger schools, creating this sense of urgency cannot be delegated. Remember; what the head deems important will become important.

In a hypothetical example, if the head's weekly meeting with the development director is mostly devoted to "stuff," then the head is communicating that the fundraising goals of the strategic plan are not that important. But if that meeting is largely devoted to new prospects, potential trustees, strategies to move forward on an ask, and other discussions that are clearly connected to the aspirations of the school, the message is loud and clear – focus your time and energy on creating value as outlined in the strategy.

Urgency also includes creating the conditions for success. Setting up a lot of committees whose members often lack appropriate expertise and yet are responsible for implementation may be what the textbook advocates. But it seems to me to be an anemic, bureaucratic management tool that sucks all the passion and accountability out of execution. Try holding a committee accountable. Trustee committees, to be sure, may need to vet ideas related to implementation, but I have witnessed too many strategic plans that have died and gone to the bookshelves because the head did not create a nimble structure for implementation. Process, though essential, can be overused to the point that it kills results.

Creating a sense of urgency does not mean being authoritarian. It means that the head is using her power to focus attention. Collaboration is still a necessary ingredient in the winning formula because it promotes honest conversations and creative solutions. Furthermore, it is the head's responsibility to ensure that implementation is not simply articulating tasks, completing them, and declaring victory. Those involved in implementation, instead, have to continually toggle between strategy, tactics, and vision.

The head is ultimately responsible for effective execution. Heads do this by being open and collaborative, asking questions while insisting that the team or individual gets to a plan of action:

"What needs to be true for the school to achieve this objective?"

"Who else needs to be brought in to execute the plan?"

"Have we examined alternative approaches?"

"Make the case that the plan will help the school achieve its stated goal?"

"How long will this take?"

"What do you need from me?"

These are just a small sample of questions that make it clear that the head wants to achieve the goal and that those responsible for implementation are not simply there to come up with a to-do list with items that can easily be checked off. Management legend Peter Drucker wrote, "Efficiency without effectiveness is meaningless." The head can ensure effectiveness by 1) paying attention, 2) asking hard questions, 3) connecting dots and getting others to do the same, 4) encouraging imagination, and 5) making it clear that the school is after real change, not just the façade of change that creates no value.

Selling- Any worthwhile vision is a bet. A huge unknown requires stakeholders to believe, to take the proverbial leap of faith. From that faith comes purpose, motivation, and action. The head's primary job in creating value for the school is to inspire stakeholders and connect their efforts to the achievement of something meaningful.

Visionary heads are constantly providing the "why." In the beginning, establishing that "why" can be a long and arduous task that may alienate some stakeholders and lead to frustration. But once established, it provides the head with a powerful tool to set guardrails and at the same time, inspire. Independent schools would be far better off if heads spent more time thinking about how an employee's work helps advance the school and ensuring that the employee knows it. The same principle applies to heads working with trustees. Selling never stops.

When I use the word "selling," I am not talking about Professor Harold Hill in *The Music Man*. It won't take long before people see through the "think system." Yet the play speaks to the need in all of us to believe that our lives make a difference. A leader helps followers see the profound meaning in their work. That meaning is inextricably connected to the realization of the dream. And because the effort resides in a belief instead of a certainty, it has the power to motivate, to get people to work harder and smarter to prove that that they, as well as the school, can achieve the impossible. To sell is to inspire. This is much different from a head presenting a PowerPoint plan that has all the moves spelled out. In this case, efficiency becomes the enemy of effectiveness.

In a previous chapter, I wrote about the importance of humility as a key tool in inviting others into the conversation and revealing new approaches. But in selling the vision and goals to stakeholders, the head must set humility aside and speak confidently. Not cockiness, but confidence. Followers are not just devoting their efforts to the dream; they are also devoting their efforts to the leader. They need to believe in the leader, so much so that they will follow her on this journey into the unknown.

The leader's role is obvious in the world of philanthropy, where major donors are not going to give unless they have confidence in her. And that confidence is often the result of the head's visibility and passionate enthusiasm for the school. Effective feasibility studies always include a section about the head for this very reason. But make no mistake, the head's confidence must be rooted in her work at the beginning of the journey, analyzing the school, understanding the competition, identifying capabilities, creating structures, figuring out a plan, and more. The head reveals confidence by demonstrating that she knows what she is talking about; she has done her homework. Just because attempting to achieve a bold vision is a bet, doesn't mean that it's a blind bet.

Thick Skin- I suppose that one of the benefits of the "vanilla" strategic plans one sees on many websites is that they lack controversy. This means that stakeholders can easily support the goals or more likely, be neutral. The head escapes the many uncomfortable situations that arise when the plan clearly requires making choices. But the downside of these "vanilla" plans is that they're not strategic. They don't solidify a market position or enhance a brand. Making choices is essential in establishing and strengthening the school's story, which, in turn, sets the table for future success.

Here is where the head's EQ and her relationships with the key stakeholders, especially the trustees, can make a difference. Understanding a trustee's hierarchy of values by listening carefully to that trustee in the first year can provide the head with an entry point for finding common ground. In addition, the head's clear understanding of why the school has chosen a certain path can engender confidence even if the stakeholder disagrees. Similarly, knowing that a trustee wants straight talk instead of smoke and mirrors helps the head devise a strategy for that kind of conversation.

EQ can mitigate the fallout of some disagreements, but at times, there is no way to avoid disagreement and sometimes, anger. In these situations, listening to understand and at the same time, being resolute in your convictions can prove helpful in ensuring that the disagreement does not lead to a permanently damaged relationship. Entering these conversations with an awareness of areas of flexibility as well as non-negotiables, helps to navigate the discussions. The worst tactic for a head is to avoid the conversation when a key stakeholder is clearly upset with the direction of the school. Heads who tend toward conflict avoidance must develop the discipline to lean into those hard conversations. Letting a key stakeholder seethe is not a winning strategy.

Delegate but … - In an earlier chapter, I discussed my propensity to micromanage in certain areas, thus disavowing a widely-held management principle. I micromanaged because I was obsessed with results in seven areas: faculty recruitment, admissions, music, development, athletics, diversity, and college placement. In these areas, I didn't just want departmental reports; I wanted to understand the nuances; I wanted to know the stories so that I could be an effective thought partner with the senior administrators — adjusting tactics, re-examining program in light of these departments' experiences, and assessing strategy at a granular level.

By way of example, it became clear to the college counselor and me in my first year that even with the limited number of highly capable students, the school needed to create an honors program in which these students pushed each other, creating a culture of excellence within their small peer group. There were about eight students in a rising 9th-grade class, who clearly had the capability of achieving academic excellence by any standard. I saw the value of bringing these students together rather than having them languish separately in classrooms that were not nearly as challenging. The strategy worked; eventually, these students attended Brown, Dartmouth, Duke, Amherst, Bowdoin, NYU, Washington University, William & Mary, and Haverford. I now had an "academic excellence" story to tell. By micromanaging, I was able to take advantage of an opportunity that helped to demonstrate that we were becoming, indeed, the school we claimed to be. In addition, I used my authority as head to drive the change so that Rivers could take advantage of the opportunity these eight students presented before it was gone.

There is a key lesson here for heads. Early in the change process, the head is often the person best able to connect the dots between vision, strategy, and tactics. In an ideal world, the key administrators would be part of a team that made these connections, allowing the head to receive regular updates on progress-to-date. I am sure this kind of management exists, but I have never witnessed it. In my experience, if the head is not in the trenches at the beginning stages in areas that are vital to the success of the strategy, then opportunities are lost.

Successful heads are obsessed with results. When they see critical pathways to achieving the desired results, they will gladly throw management protocols out the window. In my conversations with Tom Hudnut, the founding president of Harvard-Westlake, I learned about his unrelenting focus on results and his desire to pay close attention to those areas of the operation where decisions would have a significant impact. Even in a school of 1700 students, Tom "insisted on having the final word in the hiring of teachers and the admission of students." Success in these two areas was vital in realizing his vision; thus, delegating these decisions without any oversight was not an option. Tom not only hovered over critical areas that impacted results but did so in areas of his strength - faculty hiring and admissions. Herein lies another valuable lesson for new heads: know your strengths and deploy them wisely.

Risk- I know for some heads of school with risk-averse personalities, embracing risk is difficult to swallow. I understand. But to achieve something great will often require smaller leaps of faith and a larger willingness to dare. This kind of leadership reflects institutional confidence and signals to faculty and administrators that the school will be a petri dish for fresh ideas, a place where imagination is valued. A leader can't publicly value innovation and then reject the vast majority of innovative ideas that bubble up. Avoiding failure is not a recipe for transformative change. If a head wants her school to develop a culture of innovation, she will need to say "yes" more often than "no."

The intent of innovation is to help the school get closer to the realization of its vision by using the collective imagination of talented people. Innovation for the sake of innovation is worthless. Alignment matters. But if new ideas are aligned with the goals of the school, the leader's predisposition to encourage reasonable risk-taking can add enormous value to the school. One successful head often responded to new initiatives by asking, "What's the worst that could happen?" More often than not, in answering the question, it was clear that the consequences were not all that dire. But the more profound result was a culture in which educators were permitted to innovate and dream. His job was to ensure those dreams would add value to the school.

Annual Goals- Strategy is about the long game; it's about sustainable change that leads to new opportunities. During my time at Rivers, I believed fervently that one of my long-term goals was to build a recession-proof school, a school whose brand was so strong that it could easily survive a recession. To this end, the ritual of establishing annual goals made no sense. Annual goals are about the short term; I was playing the long game. Until I abandoned the exercise altogether, I would spend hours hunched over my computer, struggling to formulate goals I thought would resonate with the board. Perhaps a more facile manager would have been able to perform this annual ritual. Afterall, there is a strategic plan and from that plan should emerge the head's annual goals; it seems so logical.

But when I thought about annual goals designed to move the school closer to achieving the vision, I often drew a blank. Instead, I wanted a more organic formulation of short-term goals, one that emerged from the creativity of conversations, the new learning that results from success and failure, the changing landscape of reality, and emerging opportunities, all of which reflect a strategic perspective and none of which fit into a "nice" square box. Moreover, the time limitation of one year struck me as ridiculous. Returns on investments don't often conform to such a strict timeline. Yes, some investments returned immediate results but those investments were connected to achieving the vision, not satisfying a board that at best, wants accountability, and at worst, wants to control the head. The whole exercise seemed to be more performative than substantive.

In my work with heads whose boards require annual goals, I am appalled by some of the goals these boards inflict on their heads. Of course, the boards feel a need to create measurable goals in keeping with best management practices that hold the head accountable. A favorite one is to increase enrollment by some percentage. I cringe when I see this goal. Its effect is to divert the head's attention away from building a thriving school and instead focus her time and energy playing unproductive games to achieve the goal. Indeed, if the head decides to admit students who are not mission-appropriate, she is sacrificing the school's long-term future for a short-term win. If she gets a bonus for achieving the goal, she wins; the school loses.

In order for schools to create value, they need strategic goals that clarify the pathway to achieving the vision. Trustees should certainly play a role in the formulation of the goals. But after the vision and goals have been established, administrators and trustees should work together to realize the vision. In particular, the head and the board chair must drive the implementation of goals. This work may involve deadlines but not at the expense of excellent work and long-term sustainability. Annual head of school goals, more often than not, don't reflect a partnership in service to achieving something great. Rather, they are useless management tools designed to create the illusion that the board is properly overseeing the school by managing the head. (Olverson, November 2021, RG 175 Blog)

Learning- When I vet head of school candidates, one of the most important qualities I look for is a desire to learn. This desire is reflected in a number of behaviors — asking questions, listening carefully, changing one's mind, demonstrating humility, studying data, reading, thinking, and attending conferences. Indeed, a head needs to attend to her professional growth in order to model an important value for the school's professional community. A softer but no less important benefit of attending conferences is to connect with fellow heads who understand the pressures of the job. Conferences within the independent school world allow heads to be their authentic selves; they don't have to be "on" as they do when they're at school.

But professional learning limited to independent school conferences is entirely too constrictive.

Our industry would benefit enormously if heads found sources of learning outside the industry and used that learning in novel ways to advance their schools. In a conversation with the former vice-president of innovation at a global company, I learned that each year he brought together innovation leaders from industries outside of his, in order to share ideas in their respective domains. A head can go to independent school conferences and learn about new programs; there is nothing wrong with this. But new programs are not the same as new ways of thinking. When I exposed myself to leaders outside the school industry and learned how they thought, I could often readily see the application to my work. If Steve Jobs' quote about creativity is correct, why not break out of our insularity and learn from other industries?

For several years, I went to the systems thinking conference. From attendance at those conferences, I began to see the power of structures to influence behavior, which, in turn, gave me a powerful lens through which I could see the many ways we could better align the school's operations. From the Monitor consultant, I learned at a deeper level what drives customer behavior. Deep learning is not about one-off programs; it's about expanding the leader's view of reality and learning about new tools that can be used to unleash creativity.

A Good Laugh- "These are my principles. If you don't like them, I have others," Groucho Marx once proclaimed. Early in my tenure as a first-time head, I often wondered if the senior administrative team members laughed at my jokes because I was the head of school. After a few years, I stopped wondering. Even if they felt as if they had to laugh, I didn't mind occupying an alternative universe in which I was a funny guy. Even though the work of a team is serious, humor has a way of reminding the members that they are wonderfully human with their idiosyncrasies, their flaws, and their unique personalities. Humor gives the team permission to laugh at itself and not take itself too seriously. It tells its members that having fun while doing serious work is perfectly fine. It sets a positive mood that signals to members that they can be their true selves in front of the group. But most importantly, it demonstrates to faculty and staff that as hard as independent school work is, it can also be fun. The head has so many roles, but undoubtedly, one of the most important is that of chief mirth officer (CMO), in which she affirms the importance of laughter in maintaining morale, generating a positive community spirit, and overcoming adversity.

ions

1. What are your management tendencies? Which ones will need adjustments in order to execute effectively?

2. Will the board chair be an effective partner in implementing the strategic goals?

3. Are you prepared for the pushback you may receive as the school moves in a different direction?

4. What individual stakeholder relationships need to be strengthened before executing strategy?

5. How will you keep yourself and the stakeholders focused on the North Star?

6. Who are your key thought partners as you implement change?

7. How will you model a positive and optimistic leadership style?

8. What tasks are you spending most of your days on? Are they related to achieving the vision? Is there a need for more delegation?

Reader's Notes

Chapter 9

Epilogue

It's little wonder that conflicts have emerged between trustees and heads at many schools over the last three decades. Most trustees come from the business world, where the constantly shifting context demands responses that lead to a focus on the immediate. This is the lens through which they view schools. But sustainable change in the independent school business requires a long-term perspective. Yes, schools need to be nimble, but careening from one "hot" idea to another is not a strategy. Rod Snelling often said that sixty percent of what trustees know can be beneficial to an independent school, and the other forty percent can be incredibly destructive. I'm not sure Rod had the right percentage, but there is anecdotal evidence that trustee ignorance of the nature of the independent school business is leading to shorter head tenures.

The obvious response to this challenge is board education. A one-day workshop led by a consultant, the reasoning goes, will enlighten the trustees and change their behavior. I don't doubt some benefit from these workshops, but in general, I think they are quick fixes to a much more systemic problem. In addition, using consultants at the beginning of the head's tenure often has the unintended consequence of diminishing the head's stature and power — the bedrock for devising and implementing meaningful strategy.

Strategy in the school business is about the long game. The head is responsible for thoughtfully and intentionally leading trustees to a new and more useful perspective that puts real strategy, instead of planning, front and center. In short, if heads want to use strategy as the key component in adding value to the school, they have to create the conditions for success by shifting the trustee perspective to the strategic rather than the immediate. Once trustees assume that the school is playing the long game, they will much more readily jettison the unrealistic short-term goals that all too often sacrifice the future of the school.

With this understanding in mind, I share with you the outcomes derived from the strategic mindset Rivers used throughout my tenure and after. In keeping with the value of a long-term focus, these statistics purposely concentrate on results 15 to 25 years after establishing the initial strategic plan in 1998.

I know that hard data provides only one lens to evaluate the school, and the data I have from Rivers is limited to enrollment management, college admissions, fundraising, music, athletics, and diversity. But the success in these areas reveals the power of strategy, done right, to create value for a school over time.

Enrollment

Between 1998 and 2023, Rivers had developed and implemented three strategic plans. The first focused on the table stakes needed to ensure that Rivers effectively competed against the constellation of good and great schools in the Boston area in academics, athletics, and the arts. While maintaining a focus on excellence, the second strategic plan concentrated on the school's differentiator among these schools - humanity. The third established a campus plan and new facilities that promoted "Excellence with Humanity." The success of all three strategic plans strengthened the school's brand and resulted in a robust and sustainable enrollment with mission-appropriate students.

In 1997, the school enrolled 317 students in grades 7 to 12. The middle school had 62 students, and the upper school had 255 students. At the time, Rivers' upper school was the smallest among co-ed schools in the ISL, undoubtedly contributing to the lack of athletic success. More specifically, there were a couple of years when the football numbers were so low that the school considered abandoning the program and thus, leaving the league. Several years earlier, the ISL granted Rivers a one-year exemption from football participation because of low numbers but with the understanding that if it opted out again, it would have to leave the league.

By 2014, the school had full enrollment of 490 students, 123 in the middle school and 367 in the upper school. Over the last 25 years, Rivers has never had a decline in enrollment. In fact, enrollment increased each of those years except for two and only because of limited classroom space. Even during the 2008 financial crisis, the school increased enrollment, achieving my goal of a recession-proof school. The increases over the 25 years were gradual in keeping with the school's focus on the long term and its capacity to deliver on its mission for all students. Growth would not come at the expense of quality. As the school added classroom space, most notably a stunning STEAM building in 2021, it continued to add enrollment gradually. Today, the school has 525 students, 138 in the middle school and 387 in the upper school. This represents a 66% increase since 1997!

But enrollment growth was not primarily the result of accepting more students from a similar-sized pool. Applications increased dramatically over the 25 years. In 1998 there were 280 applications with an acceptance rate of 69%. By 2013, the number of applications had almost doubled to 557, and at the same time, the acceptance rate dropped to 37%. The school had substantial waitlists at most grade levels. In 2022 the number of applications had jumped to 730, while the acceptance rate dropped to 33%. The application numbers have held steady post-Covid. Yield over this period increased from 48% to 51%, a modest increase to be sure, but one that reflects the fierce competition for students among independent schools in Boston. Typically, yield decreases when there is a dramatic increase in applications. The fact that Rivers' yield had slightly increased meant that it was holding its own in the new market segment it was competing in.

Attrition figures also indicated that the school was delivering on its brand promise. In 1998, the school's attrition rate was 8.1%. By 2014, it had dropped to 2.3%. In recent years, attrition has ranged from 2 to 4%, well below the national average and further indication that the school's value proposition continues to be strong.

College Admissions

Admission to selective colleges is one of the most frustrating and misunderstood elements of the independent school world. The value that some parents place on admission to a highly selective college with a brand name far exceeds the real benefits these colleges provide. This value can easily devolve into a quagmire of distorted ethics, as evidenced by the Varsity Blues Scandal. Most of us in the independent school world have seen the ill effects of the pressure high-achieving students place on themselves when trying to win the golden ring of a prized college acceptance.

Despite my skeptical view of college admissions, Rivers needed to "play the game," albeit with a heavy dose of humanity. Schools can't just claim they are academically excellent; they must prove it. In Boston, that meant there had to be enough prestigious colleges on the college enrollment list to indicate that the school truly had excellence. More importantly, the school needed talented and engaged students in order to create a dynamic intellectual culture that would promote deep learning. To get these students, it had to show a clear path for them to gain admission to highly selective colleges. This was the market reality in Boston, and it was imperative that the school account for this reality. The challenge to achieve this goal was a tall order. In fact, the school, to this day, never reached its ambitious goal for college admissions in the first strategic plan. But it dramatically changed the college profile nonetheless.

The college counselor and I came up with a list of 50 colleges that we wanted fifty percent of our graduates to attend. We agreed that we would not sacrifice a student's autonomy to pressure her into applying to specific colleges. We would not distort the process or the commitment to humanity. In addition, in no way did we think these 50 colleges were the best colleges in the country. In fact, we were unconcerned about the best colleges. In choosing the colleges, we focused on what we thought would be a driver in the market. In other words, if we could have a certain percentage of students enroll in these 50 colleges, the market would begin to see Rivers as an academically excellent school. In short, what college enrollments would enhance the school's academic reputation? If Rivers were in a different part of the country, the list would be different.

Being in New England in a city with well-known institutions of higher learning, the school had a steep hill to climb. Our Top 50 list included the usual suspects of highly-regarded colleges in the Northeast, some highly selective New England small colleges, and colleges throughout the country that were viewed as prestigious. We separated 15 colleges from the list as ones that would be viewed as the very best from a marketing perspective. The top 15 included

Cornell	Yale
Dartmouth	Princeton
Harvard	Columbia
Brown	University of Pennsylvania
Stanford	Duke
MIT	California Institute of Technology
University of Chicago	Williams

Amherst.

To reiterate, neither the college counselor nor I talked about these colleges in terms of "best" as if there were some objective criteria to rate the undergraduate experience for each of them. Rather, they were chosen because the Boston public would associate enrollment in these colleges with academic excellence, eventually driving talented and engaged students to the school, helping to create our desired learning environment.

In 1999, the school graduated 62 students. Fourteen attended our Top 50 Colleges, and none attended our Top 15. In 2013, the school graduated 80 students. Thirty-seven attended our Top 50 Colleges, and 10 attended our Top 15. In 2022, Rivers graduated 94 students. In that graduating class, 43 students enrolled in the Top 50 Colleges, while 16 enrolled in the Top 15. Although the school never reached its goal of having 50% attend our Top 50 Colleges, its success placed it securely in the constellation of good and great independent schools – mission accomplished. The school had achieved its table stakes goal and could safely turn to humanity as its differentiator.

In other areas associated with college admissions, the school was quite successful. The average combined SAT score in 1998 was 1175. In 2013, it climbed to 1300; in 2023, it rose to 1450, although almost half the class does not report standardized test scores today. In 1998, 30% of AP scores in seven different subjects were 4 or 5. In 2014, 78% were 4 or 5 in 23 subjects. And in 2019, before the effects of the pandemic, 81% of AP scores were 4 or 5, again in 23 subjects.

Fundraising

When I arrived at Rivers in 1997, the school was in the middle of a small campaign to renovate the library and admissions wing. The campaign was for a little over $1 million and was floundering somewhat with a head-of-school transition. As stated earlier, the facilities at Rivers were tired and outdated. Any renovation would be a plus. Midway through my first year, the school got lucky. A trustee pledged $1 million for renovation of the science building, and this infusion reignited the library/admissions campaign. This was the school's first $1 million gift, setting a tone for philanthropy in the future.

Subsequently, within the last 23 years, the school has embarked on four capital campaigns, each one successful. In the early 2000s, Rivers raised $15.5 million for a 72,000-square-foot athletic center, including a hockey rink and gym. The rink provided a home for our boys' program and allowed us to create a girls' hockey program. The campaign included several gifts of $1 million or more, creating greater institutional confidence. In 2007, the school built a new music center in keeping with its goal of leveraging the music school to create a program of distinction for the day school. The school successfully raised $7 million to complete the project. Four years later, focusing on creating spaces that reinforce the humanity brand, Rivers embarked on a $11 million campaign for a new campus center. Several years later, under the leadership of Head of School Ned Parsons, Rivers completed its first-ever comprehensive campaign with a goal of $50 million. The campaign exceeded all expectations and ended with well over $65 million raised during a five-year period. The campaign's centerpiece was a magnificent three-story STEAM facility and a complete revamping of the campus, making it much more aesthetically pleasing and user-friendly.

None of these campaigns could have happened without a more philanthropic board of trustees, excellent teaching, a stronger brand in the Boston independent school world, and successful annual funds that stoked the spirit of giving and identified potential major donors.

In the late 1990s, the annual fund had respectable participation from parents and alumni. Seventy-eight percent of parents and 25% of alumni participated in the 1998 annual fund. During the late 90s, the school raised over $400,000 in annual giving on average. As stated earlier, the director of development and I began focusing on dollars raised instead of participation, as the school needed to fund increasing teacher salaries as the cornerstone of its strategy. It took a few years, but 2002 saw a significant jump to over $700,000 raised. From that year on, the annual fund grew substantially. In 2012, it had reached over $1.5 million, and just ten years later, it topped $2.8 million with over 90% parent participation and 37% alumni participation. In comparison, according to the *NAIS Trendbook,* 68% of day-school parents and 8% of day-school alumni participated in the annual fund nationwide in 2018.

Music

The Conservatory Program began in the early 2000s with a modest enrollment. Within 15 years, it was flourishing. One student earned an acceptance to Julliard, and two others attended the London School of Music. A fourth student won acceptance to the Columbia University-Julliard dual degree program. By 2023, Conservatory students were winning district, state, and national recognition. At the 2023 festival for the Massachusetts Instrumental and Choral Conducting Association, all three classical ensembles won the highest awards. Two individual students won gold medals at the same festival. Six classical music students were invited to the eastern regional festival, and three were invited to the national festival. Jazz students performed equally well, with two groups winning gold medals at the state competition. Twenty-one students in chamber music and jazz programs were recognized at district and state competitions. The jazz band was routinely invited to participate in the Mingus competition in New York City. Choral groups also won district and state competitions. One student wrote an original piece performed by The Rivers Conservatory Orchestra as part of the Conservatory's long-standing Contemporary Music Festival.

The impact of the Conservatory Program cannot be overstated. The school had established a program of distinction, and the program was attracting outstanding students. Many of these students attended our Top 50 Colleges, thus solidifying the school's reputation for academic excellence and contributing to its intellectual vitality. Recognizing the music school as an asset and using imagination to leverage this gem proved a winning formula.

Athletics

Early in my career, Rod Snelling told me that high school students don't brag about their English classes to their friends at other schools. But they will brag about athletic success. In addition, when athletic success is present, students, even those who don't play sports, will start wearing school sweatshirts and hats. The transformation of the athletic program at Rivers over the last 25 years has been spectacular. Before 1999, the school had won a total of 20 ISL and New England championships. In the subsequent 25 years, Rivers athletes have garnered 50 ISL and New England championships. The school is no longer considered the doormat of the league. Today, students proudly wear their team jerseys in and out of school. Several seniors earn athletic scholarships or admission to highly selective colleges based on their athletic achievements. School pride has increased dramatically. The strategy to invest in outstanding coaches paid off to a degree we could not have imagined back in 1998.

Diversity

Being in the richest town in Massachusetts with little racial or socio-economic diversity proved a major obstacle to recruiting a diverse student body. The gains the school made over a 15-year period were hard-fought and primarily due to the great work of the associate director of admissions. In 1997, the school had just under 10% students of color. By 2014, that number had jumped to 15%. As the school's reputation grew after 2014, the percentage of students of color also grew. Today, 30% of the students identify as students of color – a remarkable achievement given the headwinds the school faced. Socio-economic diversity also increased during this period. In 1999, 84 students received financial assistance. Fifteen years later, that number increased to 142; in 2022, 150 students qualified for financial assistance. Financial aid contributed to socio-economic diversity, and helped the school attract talented students who created the stories of excellence that established and solidified the school's reputation. In addition, within the last ten years, the school has established a robust DEI program that touches almost every facet of the program and has helped to create a more inclusive school culture.

Afterword

Although this book is designed to demonstrate the benefits of strategy to independent school leaders, it also represents a plea to independent school organizations to invest more in the future leadership of schools. Despite a handful of programs designed to prepare administrators for a headship, the absence of meaningful preparation for these rising stars is palpable. Recently, I completed a search for a school that purposely included out-of-the-box candidates who had enjoyed tremendous success in their previous careers but were not educators. When I vetted these candidates, using my deep-dive interview questions and reference-checking, I was struck by their multi-faceted understanding of leadership and change management, especially compared to the best candidates from the independent school world. If our industry does not invest in leadership and management training, the endless cycle of short-term failed headships and the absence of real strategy will continue.

I know that many of my illustrations came from my experience at Rivers, a school that witnessed significant change, to be sure. But the principles of strategic thinking are applicable to most independent schools no matter what stage of development they have reached. Creating a distilled vision can inspire stakeholders. Refining the school's market niche will bring clarity to the school's identity. Developing an ambitious and realistic plan can turn a vision into a reality. And assessing capabilities and management systems facilitates long-term, sustainable change. Our schools need bolder visions, no matter how secure their place in the market is. Independent schools are independent; it's time they live into the possibilities of that word.

Acknowledgments

I am so thankful for my wife Rogers who has supported me throughout the writing of this book as I recovered from foot surgery. In addition, I am grateful for the time and expertise she provided in proofreading the initial draft. I also am thankful to Tom Hudnut, former president of Harvard-Westlake School and fellow consultant at Resource Group 175. I asked Tom to provide me feedback as I was writing the book because I knew it would be helpful and honest. His insights forced me to rethink several sections of the book and helped me to clarify my thinking. I am grateful to Rob Evans, John Gulla, Heather Hoerle and Brad Entwistle who read the first draft and provided useful commentary. Jon Wasserman and Dave Lyons gathered data critical for supporting the arguments in the book.

Many people throughout my career have given me valuable counsel. More specifically, Geoff Tuff, a senior consultant at Deloitte, deepened my knowledge of marketing. I am particularly grateful for the wise counsel of key senior administrators, Gillian Lloyd, Jan Hicinbothem, Jon Wasserman, Patti Carbery, Jim Long, David Tierney, Samantha Brennan, Rick Rizoli, and Susie McGee. To the trustees of Rivers during my tenure, I express my deepest appreciation for their intelligence, experience, and generosity.

I will be ever grateful to three people who are no longer with us: Bruce Amsbary, Dan McCartney, and Rod Snelling. All three had a profound impact on my development as a leader.

Finally, I am in awe of the talented faculty and staff at Rivers who amazed me every day with their love of children, intelligence, creativity, and dedication.

About the Author

Tom Olverson is a consultant for Resource Group 175 (RG175), a firm that specializes in head of school and senior administrative searches for independent schools. Since 2014 Tom has completed over thirty searches for schools throughout the country. In addition, Tom mentors heads of school, providing timely counsel on the myriad of issues independent school leaders face. He has written numerous articles for independent school publications and introduced the RG175 blog in 2014. Before joining RG175, he headed Seabury Hall in Hawaii and The Rivers School in Massachusetts for a combined 27 years. Tom is a magna cum laude graduate of Duke University and earned his master's degree from The College of William and Mary. Tom lives in Durham, North Carolina.

Made in United States
Troutdale, OR
06/26/2024